POTATO TOTAL

Timeless Recipes for Every Home Cook

Stefan Ekengren

gestalten

T3
70
SOL
EKO
OD EKO PERLINE

Content

The potato and me

I've decided that we (that is, you) should learn more about potatoes. They're practically everywhere we look. Safe, peaceful, reliable. A culinary staple, the potato, piled up for sale in sacks, is something we've come to expect. Do we take the potato for granted, perhaps? I think we probably do. Do we deserve it? Of course we do, but what if potatoes were no longer around? Uh oh—now we're talking about a real crisis. I want to provide you with some insight, demonstrating the potato's magnitude and significance. Let's not saunter through life oblivious to one of our biggest heroes. So now let's head to the door of the potato kingdom and leap into a world of soil, starch, recipes, sun, water, harvests, and seasons.

The potato came to Europe during the 17th and 18th centuries and revolutionized history. It turned everything on its head, and old ways of thinking about how to live, farm the land, and make a living while struggling against the threat of famine all had to be reevaluated. But it was a tentative revolution. There was considerable suspicion, because potatoes were regarded as animal feed. Potatoes were first grown as an ornamental plant, with attempts being made to popularize the tuber by making alcohol from it. But once the potato replaced the groats, turnips, and rutabaga on people's plates and people learned to grow it, what happened can be described only as a revolution. A new way of life and a new path out of hunger. The potato became, and remains, an important crop and food across the globe. The potato built Europe and its population. A potato revolution!

From the outset of my life as a chef, everything has revolved around potatoes. Actually, since the moment I first began to eat everything has revolved around potatoes. When I was a kid, just like everyone else in Sweden, we ate potatoes with every meal. Potatoes and something on the side. Our commitment to it in the Ekengren home was evident, varying from homemade gratins, Hasselback potatoes, and boiled potatoes to prepackaged French fries and croquettes in the freezer for ease. The potatoes were the foundation of the meal.

When I stepped into the restaurant kitchen and started working as a chef, I saw the potato everywhere I looked. I've peeled, grated, sliced, diced, boiled, pan-fried, deep-fried, dried, and flambéed potatoes at unbridled speed since day one. The quantity of potatoes I've handled boggles the mind. Literally tons of potatoes must have passed through my hands, because I've felt each and every one. The thing is that it's all essentially done by hand. You scrape, feel, and see to the potatoes with your hands from the time they're pulled from the ground until they're on the plate. Our hands are made for potatoes and there's nothing more satisfying than peeling them.

One of my first master chefs narrowed his eyes at me during a lunch break when my inquisitive nature got the better of me. I asked him what the "secret" was to a really good dish. In reply, he drawled, "Meat, gravy, and potatoes is all the idiots want, maybe with a few side dishes." I wasn't particularly satisfied with his response. Even then I saw his point, but I wondered if there wasn't something more. Of course, I concluded that there was, after his somewhat empty but still thought-provoking answer. If you get right down to it, the food we enjoy is meat, gravy, and potatoes. But it's not the meat or the sauce in the main role. The potato, on the other hand, is something everyone is comfortable with, and we combine it with whatever else is on the plate. I love the idea of the potato as a springboard for the rest of the food we eat. Of course, sometimes we replace it with pasta or rice, but you have to admit that you're a lot more content if there's some kind of potato on your plate.

We all have our favorites when it comes to potato dishes and varieties. Like how many times have you debated which big fast-food joint has the best fries? And we all know that Mom makes the best mashed potatoes, right?! Plenty of people think that nothing but almond potatoes go with fermented herring, and I wouldn't dare contradict anyone from the north of Sweden who makes that claim! Nothing can top a tasty potato gratin, made just the way that only you make it, right? You're on safe ground here, and don't let some jerk tell you otherwise.

I've used potatoes to create many new dishes in my time. And I don't mean dishes where the potato is on the side but where it's the star. Thanks to my curiosity I cook lots of potatoes, and from this something new is born, like my take on Hasselback potatoes (see page 168). It's hard to find someone who doesn't like Hasselback potatoes, which is why I thought it would be fun (and a little risky) to do something new with it. When we were creating my fried Hasselback potatoes, I thought we'd make a crispy snack to go with bleak roe and sour cream. It was risky, but it was successful, and what a win it was!

New potatoes deserve a few words of their own—they're the crown jewels, an incredibly good seasonal vegetable that we really need celebrate. What we don't realize about new potatoes is they're only around for a short while. I wouldn't be sitting here talking about my great love for new potatoes if they were available all year round instead of a few magical weeks in the summer. Our longing for the new potato is itself a seasoning and causes us to revere it beyond all sense and measure. For me, it's the king of vegetables.

Unfortunately, there's something about new potatoes that angers me and makes my blood boil. The price! I remember one year when my family was shopping for our midsummer celebration. I was going around the store and picking out some fine Swedish produce, for which I'm happy to pay a little extra, when in a corner of the vegetable aisle I saw something I never want to see again. By the boxes of new potatoes, there was a horde of desperate people waging a veritable war. The store was trumpeting its "great deal" on new potatoes. The potatoes were going for five cents a pound, and everyone was going nuts. What an opportunity! I suppressed the impulse to shout out where everyone could stick their cheap potatoes, but it wasn't their fault. The price war over new potatoes in the lead-up to midsummer is hitting growers and the entire industry hard, and it takes months of valuable time to bring potato prices back up to a more sensible level after the initial price dumping. Talk about a hangover.

In the long term, this poses a threat to potatoes generally by risking lower quality. We consumers could vote with our feet and show that we're happy to pay a fair price. Just imagine freshly boiled new potatoes with butter and salt to accompany your herring or baked salmon. I'll gladly pay 10 dollars a pound for my midsummer new potatoes every year! They're worth it, these little pearls.

Boil the potatoes without peeling them? We see it done here and there in the busier stages of cooking—but seriously? Who wants to boil potatoes in their skins, then peel them hot to make potato dumplings? We never boil unpeeled potatoes in this book except in a few cases (which you have to look for). Scrubbed, yes, but never with all the skin still on them. That's my red line.

The potato's best friend and eternal companion is nutmeg. There's something gentle and refined about nutmeg. Potatoes seasoned with nutmeg give you that warm feeling in the stomach that's so incredibly difficult to achieve in cooking, or, for that matter, in life generally. I put nutmeg on a pedestal with just as much certainty as I put my foot down and say "no" to white pepper. That said, some recipes in the book do call for white pepper, because I'm no hater. But I've had a hard time taking to white pepper. I know it's popular, but it's just not me. Sometimes it's needed, though.

And now a few words about salt. All potatoes require salt. Although each variety is different, they all require a decent amount of salt. Although some recipes give exact measurements, you'll have to try to come up with a guide of your own for the salt. So don't forget to add salt, please.

We'll refer to the diameter of the potatoes in some of the recipes in this book, and I think it's absolutely fine to choose potatoes by size depending on what you're going to cook. Some recipes call for small potatoes and others for larger ones. No one's forcing you one way or the other, but using different sizes can help you cooking more efficiently. That said, I have respect for potatoes, and every potato that's grown should be used.

The recipes in the book are intended to serve as a basis and can be built upon and developed. Unless otherwise stated, the recipes serve four. My hope is that you'll take these recipes further, breathing new life and meaning into the potato, and adding touches that make the recipes your own. The potato is a blank canvas. It's the gold in the soil, a pearl, a gemstone, our hero during famine, and the favorite of fork mashers everywhere. It's been our savior over the centuries. The potato runs in our blood.

A

Potato varieties

Trying to delineate all the different varieties is a kamikaze mission that I do my best not to engage in. After millennia of refinement, there is a number… around 5,000, to be more precise.

The number of different potato varieties excites me hugely, just like grape varieties excite wine connoisseurs. That said, it's important that I don't make this too dramatic. This isn't something to get snobby about… it's just potatoes, after all. Although I can prattle on and on about different varieties, there are very few instances indeed where I absolutely need to use a specific variety. Most varieties work for most things. What can distinguish them is how easy they are to grow, how well they withstand being stored, their texture, and of course their flavor. When it comes to flavor, there are no marked differences, although there are small nuances. However, there is a big difference between waxy and floury varieties, so choosing the right one can be crucial!

There are also some blue and red varieties, but personally I have a hard time with the color. It makes things a little strange in almost anything you cook, so I usually don't bother with these varieties. In general, blue and red potatoes have better nutritional values, so they may be worth noting. So although they look a little strange when cooked, they're really nutritious!

In Sweden, around a hundred different varieties are grown, most of which are waxy. Here's a list of some favorite varieties. Some are classics, some are a little more exciting, and others are forgotten.

Top to bottom: King Edward, Amandine, Annika, Zoe, Gaiane.

Cherie, waxy variety. Small fine potatoes with a thin red skin. Chestnut notes in the flavor, known as the potato of love.

Connect, waxy variety. Becomes slightly floury when boiled. Pest-resistant, making it a popular organic choice. Grows deeper in the ground and tolerates drought a little better than other varieties.

Cultra, waxy variety. Red spotted variety, slightly earthy in taste. Comes from the Netherlands and fairly new to the potato scene.

Ditta, waxy variety. Starts growing late and requires warm soil. Once harvested a little later in the season, it remains really good for the rest of the year. A real classic, rough and tasty. I like to use it in potato terrine, for example (see pages 66 and 107).

Folva, waxy variety. Is happy being kept warm. Comes from Denmark. Buttery in taste and great for raw frying.

Frieslander, waxy variety. Comes early in the season. From the Netherlands. The Frieslander is from the northern part of the country. Good for making crushed potatoes and absorbs butter really well.

Gammal svensk röd, floury variety. This is actually a term for several different varieties, but it's one of the oldest we have. Red skin. Versatile, but not so good for frying, turns brown easily because it contains a lot of sugar.

Leksands vit, floury variety. Jonas Alströmer brought Leksands vit from the UK in the 18th century and we tried growing it. He didn't name it though, which probably happened in Dalarna. Slightly sweet flavor.

Maria, waxy variety. Classic new potato from Sweden. Small, chubby, and oval. Immune to potato canker, easy to grow, and gives a high yield.

Melody, waxy variety. Very low starch content. All-round potato from the Netherlands. Doesn't darken at all when boiled.

Rättviks röd, floury variety. This variety was grown by Jonas Alströmer on his farm in Nolhaga, after which it has mostly been grown in Dalarna. Lumpy with a unique appearance.

Snöboll, floury variety. Also known as British Queen. Old variety that's a real classic. Summer potato that's extra floury and suitable for making chips and French fries.

Five new potato varieties

Some varieties are earlier and more fast-growing than others, but if you want guaranteed potatoes for your midsummer herring, you should pre-sprout the potatoes before planting. Here are some of the new potato varieties I like best:

Magda, waxy variety. Very early variety, fighting with Swift to be first. Yellow flesh and nutty flavor. Gives an excellent yield.

Rocket, waxy variety. The most widely grown and biggest-selling new potato. Pest-resistant and even. A potato you can rely on.

Rosara, waxy variety. A little unusual as a new potato because of its pinky-red skin. An easy-to-grow and versatile variety that works well for a lot more than just boiling. The flesh is yellow with a good flavor and creamy texture.

Solist, waxy variety. A favorite from Germany that's very good for boiling. Yellow flesh, thin skin, and buttery taste. A must on the midsummer table.

Swift, waxy variety. Very early variety, often before Magda. Has a strong, natural potato flavor and feels very much like a seasonal vegetable.

CHE 18/25

Sparris
Gaiane
Birgit
Amandine
Blå mandel
Andean Sunside
Mandel
Zoe
Ratte

Sparris, waxy variety. Danish variety, harvested in September/October. Distinct flavor. A real delicacy of a potato that's insanely good roasted in the oven.

Gaiane, waxy variety. Early variety, related to Blå Kongo. Like all blue varieties, contains a lot of antioxidants.

Birgit, waxy variety. Reddish, slightly creamy, planted in March, April, and May. Flowers in July, August, and September.

Amandine, waxy variety. Feels like a new potato even though it isn't grown like a new potato. Grows for 8 to 12 weeks, and great to grow in a bucket.

Blå mandel, floury variety. A Swedish classic. Blue skin with a light flesh and intense flavor.

Andean Sunside, floury variety. Yellow, delicate skin and flesh. Works very well for making chips and French fries.

Mandel, floury variety. An old variety that used to often be grown in Norrland. A real favorite that's great to make chips with.

Zoe, waxy variety. Early potato that can be harvested before midsummer. Red skin and flesh. Very tasty. Rich in antioxidants, just like other red and blue varieties.

Ratte, waxy variety. Nutty flavor. Reminiscent of asparagus potatoes and incredibly popular with chefs. Extra tasty for dirty potatoes (see the recipe on page 97).

Perline, floury variety. Light-yellow skin and flesh. Round-oval shape. Summer potato that grows many tubers. Good variety to have in summer and early autumn after the new potatoes have finished.

Baby Lou, waxy variety. Gives an excellent yield. Nice, small potato with a lively and distinct flavor. Works well for boiling and roasting. A(nother) favorite.

King Edward, floury variety. A classic and one of the most common varieties. Comes from the UK. Turns green easily when growing, so earthing-up the plants is important.

Annika, waxy variety. Swedish variety with a fairly neutral flavor and therefore useful for many dishes. Is not grown farther north than Mälardalen. I use it quite often in tuttul (see recipe on page 144).

Catimini, waxy variety. Good qualities for boiling. Red-speckled skin and light-yellow flesh.

Jacky, waxy variety. Gives good yields, resistant to lead mold. Related to the Anouk variety.

Anouk, waxy/semi-waxy variety. Good beginner potatoes to grow as they're resistant to leaf mold. Works well for boiling and deep-frying.

Annabelle, waxy variety. Easy-to-grow variety from Finland. Creamy texture and very tasty nutty flavor. Perfect to serve boiled with herring. A clear favorite.

Asterix, waxy variety. Easy-to-grow variety, red skin, and light-yellow flesh. One of the most popular varieties among home growers.

Perline
Baby Lou
King Edward
Annika
Catimini
Jacky
Anouk
Annabelle
Asterix

History of the potato

The short, incredibly abridged, story about potatoes

Peru is the homeland of the potato. It all started here, and countless varieties of potato were refined over thousands of years. Consider that for 8,000 years the indigenous people of Peru cultivated, refined, and lived on potatoes before the Spanish came to the country and discovered *bapa,* as it was called in Peru. That's just mad. We seem to go around in some kind of delusion and think that the potato is originally Swedish and that we have an ancestor who really has it in their blood.

The potato has always had a strong, divine, and vital role in Peru's history, obviously as food but also culturally. It would later come to be equally revered in Europe and the rest of the world, but its journey started at the foot of the Andes. Even today, the potato is of incomparable importance in Peru. It is the mother, the father, and the air that the people breathe. It is the day, the night, the stars, and security.

In Sweden, the population was suspicious of the new tuber and it was not welcomed immediately. The potato was first grown as part of trials as a potted plant by "scientists" in Uppsala before the famous Jonas Alströmer (1685–1761) began his mission to get the potato onto our dinner tables, where it could help to combat famine, hunger, and hardship during the 18th century.

But there was considerable suspicion. One of the reasons was that potatoes grow entirely in the soil, which at that time was considered threatening and dangerous. Furthermore, the leaves of the plant are definitely not to be used for anything other than potted plants, as they're poisonous and inedible. Turnips, rutabaga, cereals, and other things also grow in the soil, but partially or completely above ground, so an important task was to remove the superstition around food that is harvested from the ground. Seen in retrospect, the timing was perfect for the potato, as famine had taken hold in the Nordic countries and the rest of Europe, forcing people to accept it.

There were two people who were especially important when these suspicions had to be overcome: Jonas Alströmer and Swedish scientist Eva Ekeblad (1724–1786). They should be honored because they put the spotlight on the potato a few decades after it was grown experimentally in Uppsala.

Alströmer, perhaps the more famous of the two, was the first in Sweden to start growing and testing potatoes with the intention of their becoming a meal ingredient.

For three years he cultivated seeds he found in Europe and at home in Sweden. He was the first to realize the nutritional value of the potato and that it could be used in cooking in many different ways. Once he had been convinced, an early form of advertising campaign followed—or rather a combination of advertising campaign, preaching, and missionary work. Alströmer began to advertise in newspapers and distributed seed potatoes for free to high-ranking people to get them started with cultivation and so that they would realize the enormous benefits of the new ingredient. He deserves all the credit for this. The potato would probably have reached this point in the end anyway, but lives were saved and many litters of children could now avoid hunger once the suspicion subsided. The potato was the help that was needed against famine.

Ekeblad was a countess who worked in a laboratory and began to develop potato flour for cooking and make-up. She also tinkered with ways to make brandy from potatoes, which was cheaper and easier than the grain that had been used before. Her discoveries opened many people's eyes to potatoes who, understandably, became a little more sympathetic. But good lord, the brandy. That was probably the straw that broke the camel's back and when many put their suspicions aside. For her discoveries, in 1748 Ekeblad become the first woman to receive a place in the Royal Swedish Academy of Sciences, which she well deserved as she played a role in giving many a better life. (Perhaps not because people drank more, but because she grabbed people's attention and helped legitimize the potato.) Over the next hundred years, the population exploded. Things calmed down a little on the war front, the art of medicine began to make great progress—and then we have the potato. Although life was getting better and better, there would be difficult years ahead.

Cultivation was slow to take hold, which didn't help in lessening suspicions. First, the plant had to adapt to Sweden's light and seasonal rhythm. Frustrated growers had to plant new seeds and replant the crop from the early varieties that came from South America. It wasn't easy, you see. It often failed and brought even greater distress when all the chips had been bet on potatoes. Those were some miserable years in Europe, with harvests failing due to both crops and the climate, and millions of people starving to death. Ireland was hit particularly hard. There they focused everything on just one variety, and when it couldn't cope with dramatic climate changes for a few years, the situation became dire. People in Sweden also starved during these years, but here people had focused on several varieties, some of which did well. Nevertheless, the situation still wasn't great, and we were forced to continue developing the potato as a product and a resource.

It wasn't until the early 19th century that the potato was accepted, could be grown effectively, and made a breakthrough on a broad front. When the wood stove was introduced, it became easier to cook potatoes at home, and more and safer recipes could be created. The potato also became tastier as it was developed. The first varieties that arrived in the 17th and 18th centuries were tougher and didn't taste great, but then breeding took off and the taste improved substantially. And so we had the potato, more important than ever. Almost every family had its own croft, which was absolutely essential. Before the age of machines, children all over the country had a potato holiday every fall. When the potatoes were to be harvested, the children simply didn't come to school, and as a result the authorities introduced the potato holiday. What a name! (It was also called the harvest holiday, but potato holiday is much nicer.) In the middle of the 20th century, the potato holiday disappeared and was eventually replaced by today's fall holiday, which occurs a little later than the potato holiday did. I think about this every fall.

The potato had a hold on us even into the 20th century. During the First World War, it gave rise to riots when the government introduced food rationing, as the availability of food was poor throughout Europe. Warring countries wanted to starve others out, which also affected Sweden. In addition, harvests failed and in Stockholm, which was densely populated, grain and other crops were scarce. On May 5, 1917, a rumor spread that a trader on Södermannagatan had stashed away a batch of potatoes that he was going to sell to his regulars. Women and starving children quickly gathered outside the store. The atmosphere became violent and the police were called in as it escalated into outright riots among these admirable women who were fighting for their children's lives. The trader admitted that he had potatoes, but that he didn't intend to sell them. The police forced him to, but the potatoes didn't go far for the by now thousands of women and children outside the store. The crowds were dispersed by force, and many women were arrested and severely punished. The so-called potato rebellion took hold and spread across the country.

Some time after the riots on Södermannagatan, tens of thousands of people, mainly women, gathered outside the Swedish parliament to demand an end to rationing. The authorities eased rationing, partly out of fear of outright revolution as had happened in Russia in February of that same year. The potato uprising and the demonstrations later became part of the democracy movement in Sweden, which in 1919 led to universal suffrage for women. The potato and strong women had written history again through (slightly violent) demonstrations in the name of the potato. It's not really that long since we had a key event with the potato at its heart.

These days, the potato is a staple that is grown with ease everywhere, from mega-sized fields around the world to buckets on hipster balconies in towns. But the road to get to this point was a winding one during the first hundred years, and it continued to be winding and a bit of a headache. The state intervened early and promoted the cultivation of potatoes for a long while. People continued in Alströmer's footsteps, distributing seed potatoes and providing help with cultivation across the country.

The potato was revolutionary, but not that easy to get your head around. The potato has become our most important crop. It has followed us and continues to do so. We all have a story with the potato. I think about how much it has helped and continues to help. How will we ever be able to thank the potato? What would we have done without it?

Floury or waxy potatoes

But let's stop and think for a second... Is it important?

Floury potatoes contain more starch than waxy potatoes, and also more dry raw material, i. e., everything that's not water in a potato. When potatoes are cooked, the dry raw material explodes, which means that the surface and contents crack apart and become crumbly and are perceived as drier.

In the past, floury potatoes were used for almost everything—from regular boiled potatoes to mashed potatoes. My memories of boiled potatoes from childhood are that floury potatoes were usually used. It is possible to cook floury potatoes well, but it's tricky and, in many situations, unfortunately not a favorite.

Nowadays, floury potatoes have been reduced to simply being "potatoes for mashing." And now let's hold up right there... Over the years I've tried to mash just about every potato that has come my way and I've reached a rock-solid conclusion: Floury potatoes are just not suitable for mash! The taste isn't good, the starch sticks in the mouth, and the texture is almost always unpleasant, mainly because more water boils its way into floury potatoes. This means that adding cream, milk, and butter doesn't have the effect I'm looking for. No, floury potatoes just aren't potatoes for mashing. I actually want to get rid of the concept of "potatoes for mashing" here and now. Waxy potatoes are always better for mashed potatoes and purée because they don't absorb as much water, there is less starch, and the mashed potatoes and purée are much smoother.

On the other hand, I want to wax lyrical about floury potatoes for everything that's supposed to be crunchy. Precisely because floury potatoes contain so much starch, they're easier to crisp than waxy potatoes. French fries, chips, roast potatoes, potato wedges. You get the idea. This is where the floury potato gets vindication from me.

You could say that waxy potatoes are more durable because they have properties that make them a more reliable friend in the kitchen. This isn't an act of war against floury potatoes, but after thousands of trials, I've reached the conclusion that waxy potatoes are more all-round and useful.

In each recipe in the book, I suggest what works best: waxy or floury. So, the answer to the question I asked at the beginning of this text is: Yes. What you choose is important, and your potato life now depends on floury or waxy potatoes.

A dear potato has many names

A crop as dear and important as the potato obviously has several different names and nicknames. It's like with our kids, our loved ones, or our most important pals... they get some weird but loving nicknames. I often hear different names for potatoes, both from guests at the restaurant and when I'm around Sweden cooking. Some incredibly lovely names pop up, not dissimilar to those found in the English language.

Spud, tater, tatties, murphy, tuber, earth apple. Can you think of any more?

Scrubbed, peeled, tourne

One thing I know a lot of people fight about is boiling potatoes with the skin on. I respect it, but I don't like it myself. It's too cumbersome to peel the potatoes once they're boiled, regardless of whether they are to be eaten as they are or you're going to make something like mashed potatoes. The benefit just doesn't outweigh the trouble, and I stand by that.

Here are three different ways I deal with potatoes in this book. Now, I don't want to be a bigot by implying that some people don't know what a peeled potato looks like, but I'll make it clear just so there is no ambiguity when the terms are mentioned in the recipes.

Scrubbed potatoes

Potatoes are scrubbed with a brush, scouring pad, or electric potato scrubber. Electric scrubbers can be purchased at most major grocery stores. Scrubbed potatoes mean that you remove only the coarsest and outermost part of the skin, and this is the method I use

the most. This makes for excellent boiled potatoes, french fries, or potato gratin.

Peeled potatoes

Your regular classic potato peeler does the job here and frees the potatoes from their skins. This is especially important when the potatoes are to be puréed or piped, as in duchess potatoes.

Tourne potatoes

An older method of making potatoes fine, such as before boiling. You cut off the short ends of the potato and cut around the whole potato in an arc to have five or seven edges. Important! This takes practice! You need nice long strokes so that there are no notches in the nice round shape. If you want a slightly stronger peel for deep-fried potato skins (see page 164) this is how you make them. Boil the tourne potatoes and deep-fry the skin the next day. Or vice versa.

Boiled

Boiled potatoes. There are plenty of dishes you can make with boiled potatoes—we're talking about the basics, the original, the old faithful. Boiling potatoes is the first thing you learn in the kitchen (or should be) and is the first thing you learn to like. One of my first memories of boiled potatoes is from when I was a child in the 70s and there was a power shortage. Because of that, my mother tried to boil the potatoes for as short a time as possible. The solution was to boil the potatoes for around five minutes, after which she would wrap the pot and its boiling contents in a bath towel, place it on a sturdy cutting board, and let the potatoes cook through with the residual heat. I like this resourceful way of boiling potatoes.

There's a lot more to talk about when it comes to boiling potatoes. Sure, it may seem like the easiest thing in the world when it comes to cooking, but it's more complex than you think. Peel or not?

Peel before or after cooking?

Boil or simmer? How much salt? When are the boiled potatoes ready? Should the water be brought to the boil before putting the potatoes in the water? A raft of questions pop up when you're faced with a potato that needs to be boiled. So, here comes the most important chapter in the book—boiled potatoes.

New potatoes

There's nothing that we await more eagerly than the first nice new potato that has been carefully boiled to perfection and served with butter. It is the story of seasons, earthy fingers, and longing, and something that can only be eaten for a short time in the summer. For me, this is the most powerful potato of them all—the most powerful vegetable, in fact. New potatoes are a seasonal vegetable and should also be treated as such and cooked with the same precision as any baby carrot or beetroot. I boil water and salt, put the potatoes in, lower the heat, and let the potatoes simmer. I eat them with nothing but butter. Then I come up with a few accompaniments and dip the little seasonal gems in hollandaise sauce (sinful and completely wonderful) or eat them freshly boiled with a piece of herring.

Even more sinful is my new go-to dish—boiled new potatoes on a plate draped with béarnaise sauce and topped with pan-fried potatoes (see page 128). Everything that's right on one plate.

1 ¾ lb. (800 g) new potatoes, roughly 3 inches (7–8 cm) in diameter, scrubbed
4 cups (1 l) water
3 tsp. salt

Measure the water and salt into a pot, add the potatoes, and bring to a boil. Lower the heat and simmer in gently bubbling water for about 15 to 20 minutes, until a small hard core remains in the center of each potato.

Drain the water, put some paper towel on top of the potatoes, and allow the steam to evaporate. Place the lid back on when serving.

Allow the steam to evaporate and serve immediately.

I enjoy boiled potatoes the most when they're served alongside boiled cod with egg sauce, beef stew, or dried fish with white sauce, peas, and crispy bacon.

Boiled potatoes

"Regular" boiled potatoes that we eat with a number of everyday dishes. Firstly, use waxy potatoes. I also almost always select smaller, old potatoes when I have to boil potatoes. Large potatoes are never really good when boiled.

I always scrub my potatoes, and it's easy if you have a small machine. A brush works fine, too, but a machine makes things incredibly efficient and convenient. I only want to remove the roughest part of the skin, no matter what potato I'm boiling. Never peel all the skin off completely if you're "just" boiling potatoes. There are several reasons for this. Firstly, a lot of the potato is lost when it's peeled, and secondly, the potatoes will be fleshier if they're boiled with part of the skin left on. They hold together better and the water doesn't penetrate to the same extent as when they're peeled completely. Thirdly, there are a lot of nutrients in the skin.

Salt. It's a good idea to quickly find a way of measuring the perfect amount of salt. I have my salt quantities etched into my brain. There's nothing worse than an unsalted boiled potato, and nothing beats a perfectly salted boiled potato. It's out of this world.

Boil. No, rather simmer or lightly bubble. Vigorous boiling is not good. There's a risk that too much water will boil into the potatoes if the water boils too violently. The potatoes should simmer until they have a small, slightly hard core left in the middle which isn't completely cooked through. When the water is drained, allow the potatoes to stand and steam for a few minutes until they're completely cooked. You have to get a feel for when there's a little core left in the center of the potato. If you can, always use the same knife or skewer, which you're already familiar with, when boiling potatoes, as then you'll get to know the feeling. Yes, you heard it here. Boiling potatoes is anything but simple or something you could do in your sleep. The recipe alongside may seem simple, but as you may have realized by now, there's a lot to think about after all.

1 ¾ lb. (800 g) waxy potatoes, roughly 3 inches (7–8 cm) in diameter, scrubbed
4 cups (1 l) water
3 tsp. salt

Measure the water and salt into a pot, add the potatoes, and bring to a boil. Lower the heat and simmer in gently bubbling water for about 20 minutes until a small hard core remains in the center of each potato.

Drain the water, put some paper towel on top of the potatoes, and allow the steam to evaporate. Place the lid back on when serving.

Fork-mashed potatoes with Sandefjord sauce, trout roe, and dill.

Pressed potatoes

The arch nemesis of fork-mashed potatoes—pressed potatoes. If you ask fork-mashed potatoes, pressed potatoes are redundant—"You do it with your fork on the plate!" Despite being the patron saint of the fork-mashed potato, I now rush to the defense. Pressed potatoes are insanely good and completely different from fork-mashed.

It's important that the potatoes are pressed and served when they're piping hot and freshly boiled, because if left to steep, the starch develops in the potatoes and they can become sticky. But also because of that unbeatable feeling of a steaming bowl of freshly pressed potatoes on the dinner table. Just like fork-mashed, it's important to have a lot of sauce. If there's too little, then just don't even bother. The sauce should be absorbed by the potatoes. It'll all just fail without enough sauce. I always top the bowl of freshly pressed potatoes with a few knobs of butter, which melts into them and takes them to another level. A few flakes of salt and some black pepper are also good.

One tip is to put the pot of potatoes on the table, put out a potato press and let everyone press their own potatoes directly on their own plate, maybe for cabbage dolmas or a beef bourguignon? Cozy, but it can get a little messy (all in the name of art)!

1 ¾ lb. (800 g) waxy or floury potatoes
4 cups (1 l) water
3 tsp. salt
½ stick (50 g) butter
Salt flakes
Freshly ground black pepper

Measure the water and salt into a pot, add the potatoes, and bring to a boil. Lower the heat and simmer in gently bubbling water for about 20 minutes, until a small hard core remains in the center of each potato. Drain the water and allow the steam to evaporate for a minute.

Press the potatoes straight into a bowl. Spread butter on top, sprinkle in some salt flakes and ground pepper. Serve immediately.

Crushed potatoes

Now we start adding things to the boiled potatoes to enhance them and add extra dimensions and perspectives to the natural potato flavor. What I like about crushed potatoes is that they feel sloppy, rough, and a bit rushed. But don't be fooled, there's cooking and precision involved here as well.

The crushing itself is best done with a potato masher, but a quick crush with a balloon whisk, wooden spoon, or fork also works well. Just press crush on! Most important in my crushed potatoes are lots of finely chopped onions that have been cooked until soft in lightly browned butter. But only lightly browned. If they're browned too much, it overpowers the flavor and colors the crushed potatoes too much. Parsley and dill are also important. Neither milk nor cream is used in crushed potatoes, only the butter from stewing the onions.

I love crushed potatoes for poached fish with a good sauce and for grilling in the summer. This is a favorite of mine that works well with so much.

1 ¾ lb. (800 g) waxy or floury potatoes, roughly 3 inches (7–8 cm) in diameter, scrubbed
4 cups (1 l) water
3 tsp. salt
1 stick (100 g) butter, lightly browned and cooled
4 banana shallots, finely chopped
Zest of 1 lemon, grated
1 bunch dill, coarsely chopped
1 bunch parsley, coarsely chopped
Salt and freshly ground black pepper

Place the browned butter and onion in a pan. Let the onion soften in the butter on a low heat for about 15 minutes.

Measure the water and salt into a pot, add the potatoes, and bring to a boil. Lower the heat and simmer in gently bubbling water for about 20 minutes. Drain the water and allow the steam to evaporate for a minute.

Pour in the butter and onion mixture and mash the potatoes quickly. Fold in the lemon zest, dill, and parsley. Season with salt and pepper to taste.

Previous page, left to right: crushed potatoes, mashed potatoes, potato purée.

Fork-mashed potatoes

Let's move on to different variants of the basic boiled potato and the most important and tastiest of them all—the fork-mashed potato. For a child in Sweden, it was a matter of course and nothing to be ashamed of. With purpose and gusto, you mash the potatoes in the sauce without anyone thinking that you're rude or have poor table manners. When you grow up, this way of consuming potatoes is abandoned. It's not considered "nice" to mash them with a fork, and that only the deranged and food terrorists serve mashed potatoes where boiled potatoes would have been much better. I call for a revolution! Can't everyone just mash with a fork? From the smallest kids to construction workers, from business people in a gastro pub to the king and queen themselves. (If they don't already?)

But we hardly need a recipe for fork-mashed potatoes, right? Well, a helping hand might be needed here for those who've lost themselves in the orderliness of adult life. Let's let our hair down for a minute and channel our inner child. Never mashed with a fork? It's your time to shine.

Boiled waxy potato dish with sauce

You have a plate in front of you. Arrange the food and the sauce and place the potatoes in the sauce. Take a fork in one hand and push it through the potato completely, one or more times per potato. They shouldn't be too mashed but should absorb just enough of the sauce. Pull and turn the fork-mashed potatoes through the sauce. Eat immediately.

Mashed potatoes

Mashed potatoes are an extension and dramatically raise the tempo of crushed potatoes. Here, we use an electric whisk, or, much better, a balloon whisk, to whip the sense out of the freshly boiled potatoes. There should be a few chunks left in the mashed potatoes so they should not be pressed. Now we also start adding milk and cream. I always use both.

If you can't imagine cream in your mashed potatoes, you might as well just make pressed (see page 33) or crushed potatoes (see page 36). Mashed potatoes are something you treat yourself to. They're not a punishment. So, skip the self-torture with mashed potatoes made with only milk.

Here the nutmeg makes its entrance, the most important spice, which elevates the flavor up to the heavens. However, use it sensibly so it doesn't become too perfumey. It's easy to get carried away by the fantastic aroma when you grate the nutmeg, but try to restrain yourself.

But there's one thing that seems silly and that I don't understand—people who sugar their mashed potatoes. Potatoes contain natural sugars and, so far, I've never come across a single potato that doesn't have enough sweetness in itself. So, it's a hard "no" from me to sugar in mashed potatoes and purée (see opposite page).

1 ¾ lb. (800 g) waxy potatoes, roughly 3 inches (7–8 cm) in diameter, peeled or scrubbed
4 cups (1 l) water
3 tsp. salt
½ cup (100 ml) heavy cream
½ cup (100 ml) whole milk
1 stick (100 g) butter
Freshly ground nutmeg
Salt

Measure the water and salt into a pot, add the potatoes, and bring to a boil. Lower the heat and simmer in gently bubbling water for about 20 minutes. Drain the water and allow the steam to evaporate for a minute.

Boil the cream and milk while the potatoes cook—keep warm.

Vigorously mash and beat the potatoes. Pour in the milk and cream mixture along with the butter and mash together until smooth. Season with nutmeg and salt.

Imagine some tasty mashed potatoes with meat patties with onions. Just toss everything with the sauce, onion, and mince. The thought drives me crazy.

Puréed potatoes

There's a difference between puréed and mashed potatoes. In restaurants, purée is served more often than mash. Diners expect a smooth, fine, slightly loose purée, in which the potatoes are first pressed or passed through a potato ricer, with more cream, milk, and butter than you'd find in mashed potatoes. That, in a nutshell, is the difference between mashed and puréed potatoes.

With a purée, it's important not to boil the potatoes too long, so they don't absorb too much water. Otherwise there's not enough space for the cream, milk, and butter. The potatoes should be just about done and then passed immediately through a press or ricer and whipped until fluffy before being mixed with the dairy products.

Historically, there are examples of great chefs who have dissected puréed potatoes by first selecting the optimal potato variety, then cultivating it, and then having a method to push crazy amounts of butter and cream into the purée for maximum luxury and supreme taste. That's nice, but it can become a bit much. You begin to wonder where the potatoes are. It could be just any puréed vegetable when the proportion of potato is almost down to nothing.

The ultimate hedonist's companion for mashed potatoes is a burger. Jeez, what a calorie bomb! But also, jeez, what a feast for the taste buds!

1 ¾ lb. (800 g) waxy potatoes, roughly 3 inches (7–8 cm) in diameter, peeled or scrubbed
4 cups (1 l) water
3 tsp. salt
1 cup (200 ml) heavy cream
1 cup (200 ml) whole milk
2 sticks (200 g) butter
Freshly ground nutmeg
Salt

Measure the water and salt into a pot, add the potatoes, and bring to a boil. Lower the heat and simmer in gently bubbling water for about 20 minutes. Drain the water and allow the steam to evaporate for a minute.

Boil the cream and milk while the potatoes cook—keep warm.

Pass the potatoes through a press, strainer, or ricer and quickly whip together using a balloon whisk. Pour in the milk and cream mixture along with the butter and mix into a nice fluffy purée. Season with nutmeg and salt.

Duchess potatoes

One of the more forgotten potato options is duchess potatoes. When I started working as a chef, it would begin to form part of your DNA. I think I have some 25 different (but more or less the same) recipes for the "perfect" duchess potatoes. Diligently and greedily, I hunted down the ultimate recipe before suddenly, all the restaurants stopped making duchess potatoes! Life, eh?

A good duchess mix should be easy to pipe and must not contain chunks that can get stuck in the bag. The egg yolk adds color, flavor, and fat to the duchess potatoes, but they need the help of butter to make them really tasty. However, make sure you don't add too much butter, which can make the duchess mix loose. The pretty patterns you get from the piping bag should hold up even after baking, so this isn't something you should play around with.

Fish gratin is where duchess potatoes truly shine. We're talking about a true classic. There are two important details that elevate your fish gratin. I always add vegetables to the gratin as well. I have spinach under the fish and leek on top. Oh, and one more thing. Always quickly stew the shrimp shells yourself. It's incredibly simple and worthwhile.

1 ¾ lb. (800 g) waxy potatoes, peeled
4 cups (1 l) water
3 egg yolks
½ stick (50 g) butter
Salt

Boil the potatoes in salted water until done. Drain the water and allow the steam to evaporate for a minute.

Press the potatoes and fold in the egg yolks and butter. Season with salt to taste. Fill a cloth piping bag with potatoes and pipe while the potatoes are still a little warm as they're more pliable. Pipe into swirls or on top of a fish gratin and bake in the middle of the oven at 350 °F (180 °C) for around 15 minutes.

Fish gratin

20 oz. (600 g) fish, e.g., 10 oz. (300 g) cod fillet + 10 oz. (300 g) salmon fillet
18 oz. (500 g) prawns with shell, shell for sauce and tails for garnish
½ carrot, finely chopped
3 banana shallots, finely chopped
1 clove of garlic, finely chopped
½ stick + ⅓ stick + ¼ stick (50 g + 30 g + 25 g) butter
2 tbsp. wheat flour
1 tbsp. tomato purée
½ cup (100 ml) whole milk
1 ½ cups (300 ml) heavy cream
3 tbsp. cognac
8 oz. (200 g) leaf spinach
1 leek, roughly chopped
1 piping bag of duchess potato mix
1 bunch dill, coarsely chopped
Nutmeg, freshly grated
Salt

Sprinkle a little salt on both sides of the fish, rub the salt in and marinate at room temperature for about 15 minutes.

Sauté the prawn shells, carrot, 2 shallots and garlic in ½ stick (50 g) of butter. Liquid will form in the pan, so continue sautéing until all the liquid has disappeared and it starts to sauté again. Add flour and tomato purée and allow to sauté for a few more seconds.

Add milk and cream, leave to boil on a low heat for 10 minutes. Strain and season with salt and cognac. Check the thickness—the sauce should be the consistency of a stew.

Sauté the spinach and ½ shallot in ⅓ stick (30 g) of butter, season with nutmeg and salt. Squeeze out any excess liquid through a strainer and let cool.

Sauté the leek and ½ shallot in ¼ stick (25 g) of butter for a few minutes. Season with nutmeg and salt, allow to cool.

Set the oven to 435 °F (225 °C) fan.

Pipe the duchess mix around the edge of an ovenproof dish approximately 8×10 inches (25×20 cm) in size. Layer the base with the spinach so that it covers the entire bottom, then add the fish and leek. Spoon over the hot shrimp stew and bake in the middle of the oven for about 15 minutes. Remove the gratin and garnish with shrimp tails and dill.

Got some sauce left over? Serve it on the side—there can NEVER be too much sauce!

Stewed potatoes in white sauce

Stewed potatoes are strongly associated with two specific dishes—marinated salmon and isterband lard sausage. Do you eat stewed potatoes with anything else? In general, it can be difficult when it's so limited, but also lovely. There are, to put it mildly, enough potato varieties to choose from for other dishes that stewed potatoes can just belong to marinated salmon and isterband lard sausages.

You might think this is just a white sauce with boiled potato chunks and dill, but it's much more than that, of course. The sauce must have the right thickness, and by that I mean that it needs to be sorted before the potatoes go in. Potatoes (depending on the variety and season) cook differently, so it's important to take that into account if you want a perfect creamy stew. And there mustn't be too little sauce either. I don't know what's worse ... a stew that's too thick or one that's too runny. You need to get the ratio between sauce and potatoes right, so follow the recipe!

And yes, I use dill stewed potatoes for both salmon and isterband lard sausage.

1 ¾ lb. (800 g) waxy potatoes, ideally Annabelle, roughly 3 inches (7–8 cm) in diameter, scrubbed
4 cups (1 l) water
3 tsp. salt
⅛ stick (10 g) butter
1 tbsp. wheat flour
1 ¼ cup (250 ml) heavy cream
¾ cup (150 ml) whole milk
Zest of ½ lemon, grated
½ large bunch of dill, roughly chopped
Freshly ground nutmeg
Salt

Measure the water and salt into a pot, add the potatoes, and bring to a boil. Lower the heat and simmer in gently bubbling water for about 20 minutes. Drain the water, let the steam evaporate from the potatoes for a minute, and cool completely.

Cut the potatoes into rough pieces. Melt the butter in a pan and stir in the flour. Add cream, milk, and lemon zest. Bring to a boil and allow to boil gently for a few minutes.

Season with nutmeg and salt.

When serving: Boil the sauce again, add the potatoes, and let everything heat up. Add the dill just before serving.

Marinated salmon

18 oz. (500 g) salmon fillet
¼ cup (60 g) salt
2 tbsp. granulated sugar
Zest of ½ lemon, grated
½ large bunch of dill, in pieces

Rub salt, sugar, and lemon zest onto the salmon. Place the salmon and dill in a plastic bag and leave at room temperature for a few hours so that both the salt and sugar melt and the curing starts.

Let the salmon marinate in the refrigerator for 1 to 2 days, depending on how well-marinated you want it. I like fairly lightly marinated salmon, so I'm happy with just 1 day.

Remove the dill, dry the salmon, and slice it roughly.

For extra luxury, top with some bleak roe and butter-fried bread croutons when serving.

Scanian potatoes

Scanian potatoes—a sharper, tastier, and sturdier version of stewed potatoes that's more fun. There are countless variations, of course, and no doubt some people will want to offer up some pointers after they've read this. Dice the potatoes and sauté them quickly in a pan with lots of yellow onions and browned butter. Sweat a dash of mustard for a few seconds, then add the cream and veal stock. Let everything boil until the potatoes are just ready and then add the parsley.

It's very important to have mustard and stock in the potatoes. Of course, just cream can be good, but stock and mustard make this a potato dish that can be served on its own or as a perfect accompaniment to isterband lard sausage, beef brisket, or even broiled gravlax.

1 ¾ lb. (800 g) waxy potatoes, ideally Annika, scrubbed and cut into ½-inch (1-cm) cubes
2 yellow onions, finely chopped
⅓ stick (30 g) butter, browned
1 cup (200 ml) veal broth
2 tbsp. coarse Scanian mustard
½ cup (100 ml) heavy cream
½ bunch of parsley, coarsely chopped
Salt and freshly ground black pepper

Sauté potatoes and onions in browned butter for a few minutes in a pan.

Pour in the broth and mustard and allow to boil slowly for about 10 minutes.

Add the cream and boil for another 10 minutes. Season with salt and pepper to taste and finish off with parsley.

Brandade

Brandade, or rather "brandade de morue," is a gratinated mashed potato that is mainly made in France and can be found throughout Southern Europe. There are countless takes on brandade and each small village or region has its own. In short, it's boiled potatoes that are mashed and whipped with olive oil, garlic, bacalao (hard-salted ling or cod that has been dried) or just marinated white fish, such as haddock or cod. This is my starting point when I make brandade, but it gets a bit boring with "only" marinated fish, so I smoke it first. I also think it's too earthy with just olive oil, so I use butter and cream in mine as well. Then I don't gratinate my brandade, but just grate Parmesan over it before serving. It's important to add garlic, lemon zest, and plenty of smoked fish. Without some punchy flavors, it can easily become baby food. In France, brandade is eaten on toasted or grilled bread and I've no reason not to recommend that you do the same. I like to top it with a little bleak roe as well, to add some luxury.

8 oz. (200 g) cod fillet
2 tsp. + 2 tsp. salt
½ tbsp. granulated sugar
¼ cup (50 ml) olive oil
2 banana shallots, finely chopped
4 cloves of garlic, finely grated
1 ½ lb. (600 g) floury potatoes, roughly 3 inches (7–8 cm) in diameter, peeled or scrubbed
4 cups (1 l) water
½ cup (100 ml) heavy cream
½ stick (50 g) butter
Zest and juice of 1 lemon
Olive oil
2 oz. (50 g) Parmesan, shaved

Salt (2 tbsp.) and sugar the cod all around and leave it to rest under plastic wrap at room temperature for about an hour.

Rinse off the excess salt and sugar mixture and dry the fish well with paper towels.

Rub the fish with a little olive oil and hot smoke it in a smoker or grill for about 30 minutes. If the fish isn't ready, finish it in the oven and let it cool completely.

Mash or chop the smoked fish.

Sauté the onion, garlic, and lemon zest in olive oil over a low heat until the onion is soft—keep warm.

Measure the water and 2 tbsp. salt into a pot, add the potatoes, and bring to a boil. Lower the heat and simmer in gently bubbling water for about 20 minutes. Drain the water and allow the steam to evaporate for a minute.

Boil the cream while the potatoes cook—keep warm.

Pass the potatoes through a press, strainer, or ricer and quickly whip together using a balloon whisk. Pour in the cream, butter, and onion mixture with the olive oil. Add the fish and whisk into a nice and airy brandade. Season with salt and lemon juice to taste.

Pour into bowls or do as in France and serve on buttered toasted bread. Drizzle with a little olive oil, sprinkle with Parmesan, and serve with toasted bread.

Potato salad

Anyone who didn't eat their first potato salad in the form of a ready-made industrially prepared one, raise your hand! Thought so. I can vehemently guarantee this was the first potato salad you ate. It was definitely the case for me, at least. But I loved it, so when my mom got around to making her own, it took some time before I started to like it. I still buy ready-made occasionally, for nostalgia's sake if nothing else. But now, 99.9 percent of the time I make my own. Potato salad is a watershed moment. Do you like it creamy with mayo and crème fraiche as a base, or do you prefer it "nude," with just with vinaigrette? Without wanting to complicate things, it depends what you're going to eat with it. I like the creamy kind for cold dishes and nude for hot accompaniments. I always put finely chopped pickles and capers in my creamy potato salad, as it adds some crunch and dimension. In my nude salad, I always use pickled onions, diced iceberg lettuce, and capers to give it that little extra kick. Then I mix the nude salad with a mixed green-and-go dressing with lots of flavor from tarragon, parsley, and Dijon mustard. Picnic blanket, grilled chicken, or roast beef and potato salad. A student event or any kind of buffet—that's the place for a potato salad.

Nude potato salad

1 ¾ lb. (800 g) waxy potatoes, ideally Amandine, roughly 3 inches (7–8 cm) in diameter, scrubbed
4 cups (1 l) water
3 tsp. salt
1 clove of garlic, finely grated
2 tbsp. Dijon mustard
1 tsp. honey
2 tbsp. champagne or white wine vinegar
½ bunch tarragon, finely grated
1 bunch parsley, finely grated
4 tbsp. olive oil
4 tbsp. canola oil
¾ oz. (20 g) Parmesan, grated
Grated zest of 1 lemon
2 shallots, sliced
½ cup (90 g) pickled onion
¼ iceberg lettuce, cut into 1-inch (2-cm) pieces
¼ cup (50 g) capers with stem, halved
Salt

Measure the water and salt into a pot, add the potatoes, and bring to a boil. Lower the heat and simmer in gently bubbling water for about 20 minutes.

Drain the water, let the steam evaporate from the potatoes for a minute, and cool completely.

Cut the potatoes into rough pieces. Mix the garlic, mustard, honey, vinegar, tarragon, parsley, and oils into a green oil. Pour into a bowl and fold in the Parmesan and lemon zest.

Mix the potatoes, shallots, pickled onions, iceberg lettuce, and capers in a bowl. Fold in the tarragon oil.

Serve at room temperature.

Creamy potato salad

1 ¾ lb. (800 g) waxy potatoes, ideally Amandine, roughly 3 inches (7–8 cm) in diameter, scrubbed
4 cups (1 l) water
3 tsp. salt
2 egg yolks
2 tbsp. Dijon mustard
1 tbsp. white wine vinegar
Grated zest of 1 lemon and squeezed juice
1 cup (200 ml) canola oil
1 bunch scallions, finely sliced
1 pickle, finely diced
¼ cup (30 g) capers, coarsely chopped
1 bunch dill or parsley, coarsely chopped
Salt

Measure the water and salt into a pot, add the potatoes, and bring to a boil. Lower the heat and simmer in gently bubbling water for about 20 minutes.

Drain the water, let the steam evaporate from the potatoes for a minute, and cool completely.

Cut the potatoes into rough pieces.

Whisk together the egg yolks, mustard, vinegar, and lemon zest in a bowl. Add the oil in a thin stream while constantly whisking. Season to taste with salt and lemon juice if you want extra acidity.

Mix the potatoes, scallions, cucumber, capers, and dill in a bowl. Add the mayonnaise and mix quickly.

Serve at room temperature.

Potato dumplings

Meat soup with dumplings is one of Sweden's great classic dishes. But opinion is divided somewhat over what the dumplings should contain. Many would probably say no potatoes, so just flour and eggs with seasoning. I like dumplings with potatoes, which is how it's been done since time immemorial and is nothing new. They'll turn out a bit like gnocchi, but not quite.

¾ lb. (400 g) waxy potatoes, peeled
4 cups (1 l) water
1 ½ tsp. salt
2 eggs
3 tbsp. wheat flour
2 oz. (50 g) grated mature cheese
Salt

Boil the potatoes in salted water and press them straight into a bowl. Mix in the eggs, flour, and cheese.

Shape nice irregular dumplings with a spoon directly in a meat soup, or in boiling water if you want to make them before you make the soup.

They'll be tastier if they're allowed to simmer in the soup. The dumplings are ready when they float to the surface.

Meat soup with dumplings

1 ¾ lb. (800 g) fresh whole beef brisket or prime rib
1 bay leaf
1 tsp. salt
1 ½ – 4 sprigs of thyme
1 ½ tsp. whole allspice
1 ½ carrots, peeled
1 ½ parsnips, peeled
½ celeriac, peeled
1 ½ yellow onions, peeled
½ leek, washed
1 batch of potato dumplings
½ – 1 bunch of parsley, coarsely chopped
Salt

Place the meat in a pot. Fill with cold water so it covers the meat well and carefully add salt. Boil and skim off the top.

Add the bay leaf, thyme, and allspice and cook for about an hour before adding the vegetables (wait with the leeks). Allow to boil for another hour and add the leeks for the last 15 minutes. The total cooking time is therefore around 2 hours.

Remove the meat and vegetables and allow to cool slightly before cutting into fine pieces, large enough to eat with a spoon. Save the broth in the saucepan. Place the meat, vegetables, and dumplings in a soup bowl or in the dish from which the soup is to be served.

Boil the broth, season with salt to taste, and pour over the meat, vegetables, and dumplings. Sprinkle the parsley on top, stir and serve.

Lobscouse

I feel that lobscouse is a completely misunderstood dish, understandably. A lot of people were probably given lobscouse at school in Sweden, where it consisted of mashed potatoes with some finely chopped, boiled marinated meat. I loved it as a kid, and as I've gotten older, I've "developed" the dish further. It's needed, despite the school meal already being pretty decent. In adulthood, and with countless servings of lobscouse behind me, I've settled on boiling the potatoes in beef broth with lots of onions and chunks of marinated beef brisket. Everything is mashed with a potato masher or fork and mixed with butter and parsley. The lobscouse is thick with beef brisket, beef broth, and butter—go big or go home.

Made this way, preferably in the company of pickled beets and pickles, we're talking about a flavor bomb that can be served at any reputable three-star eatery.

2 yellow onions, finely chopped
½ stick (50 g) butter, browned
1 ¾ lb. (800 g) waxy potatoes, scrubbed and cut into rough pieces
17 oz. (480 g) marinated boiled beef brisket in pieces—see the recipe on page 72
6 cups (500 ml) beef broth
½ bunch of parsley, coarsely chopped
Freshly grounded nutmeg
Salt

Sauté the onion in the browned butter in a large pan until soft. Add the potatoes, meat, and broth and boil until the potatoes are really soft.

Mash everything with a whisk or fork. Season with salt and nutmeg to taste and finish off with parsley.

Serve with beets and pickles.

Löksälta

Löksälta is a specialty from the Norrland region of Sweden and is made from almond potatoes. The secret here is something so simple that becomes so incredibly tasty that you float off in a trance of new potato heaven. I boil new potatoes and chop shallots (yellow onions are the original, but I like shallots better) and chives, which I place in four cups together with melted butter and a little cooking water from the potatoes. Add a little extra salt to each cup, too, because the saltiness is important. Let it sit a while before it's time to serve.

I put steaming potatoes on a board in the middle of the table and mash them lightly with a fork. The guests each take a fork and dip the potato into their cup and let the flavors absorb into the potato. I leave the potatoes to sit in the cup for a few more seconds before I close my eyes, open my mouth, and take my dripping mouthfuls. All that's left is to drink from the cup for a little extra joie de vivre.

4 appetizer servings

14 oz. (400 g) small new potatoes, scrubbed
2 ½ cups (500 ml) water
1 ½ tsp. salt
1 stick (100 g) butter
1 shallot, finely chopped
½ bunch chives, finely chopped
Salt

Boil the water and salt. Add the potatoes, bring back to the boil, and reduce the heat. Simmer and bubble until the potatoes are just done, which will take around 15 minutes. Drain the water (save some and keep it warm) and let the steam evaporate from the potatoes.

Melt the butter. Divide butter, onion, and chives into four cups. Put a little of the boiling water in each cup (everyone can add their own extra salt) and let it steep for a few minutes.

Place the steaming hot potatoes on a cutting board, press lightly with a fork, and let each person take a potato with their own fork and dip it into their cup.

Papas arrugadas

This potato is prepared in the Canary Islands and is so special that it just has to be included in the book. Boiling in such an unimaginable amount of salt makes the surface of the potatoes crispy, while the potatoes themselves are not as salty as you might think. In the old days, they used sea water for boiling, which I've tried when I've visited saltier waters than what we have here in the Nordics, and it works just fine. But I still think that a little more salt than is found in natural seawater is needed for this particular dish.

When the potatoes are fully boiled, pour off all the water and put the pan back on the stove without the lid. Increase the heat slightly and let the last of the water evaporate. Keep the pot on the stove when you shake it and let the potatoes dry and the salt seep out so that the potatoes go white and crispy.

Dip in traditional mojo rojo and we're talking holiday potatoes! Unfortunately, this recipe doesn't work so well with new potatoes, as they absorb the salt in a different way.

1 ¾ lb. (800 g) small waxy potatoes, washed with skins on
9 oz. (250 g) salt
Water

Put the potatoes and salt in a pan, mix, and cover with water. Bring to a boil, lower the heat, and let the potatoes boil just until done.

Pour off the water, place the pan on the stove, and increase the heat. Shake the potatoes and let them dry until their skin is wrinkled and the salt colors it almost completely white. Serve immediately with dipping sauce.

Mojo rojo

3 tomatoes (around ½ lb./250 g), diced
½ red chili, roughly chopped
1 slice of white bread, crust removed and diced
Grated zest of 1 lemon and 3 tbsp. of lemon juice
3 cloves garlic, grated
8 oz. (200 g) grilled and peeled paprika, ready prepared in oil works well
½ pinch cayenne pepper
¼ cup (50 ml) olive oil
Salt

Quickly blend the tomatoes, chili, bread, lemon, garlic, paprika, and cayenne in a blender. Continue mixing and add the oil in a fine stream.

Season with salt to taste.

FOKER

Vichyssoise, potato soup with leeks

One of the greatest classics when it comes to soups, or really one of the greatest classics in general. And if we're stopping at classics, then we're also stopping at the mistreated and strange variations of this soup that have flourished in the world of cuisine over the years.

It's strange, actually, because it's so incredibly easy to make. Maybe it's just so stupidly simple that people feel they have to meddle with it for their own enjoyment?

But that's not what we're going to do here. The soup should be smooth, fine, and have a clear flavor of leeks and potatoes. No strange seasonings—leeks, potatoes, broth, and cream are the cornerstones here, but I also put in lots of shallots and a little bit of garlic for extra depth. Sometimes the soup seems to shimmer green, which is when you realize you've added spinach. Okay, I'll allow it. After all, we eat with our eyes, too.

And so we come to the watershed moment... hot or cold?

I prefer it cold with prawns, crème fraiche, and dill. I think that the potatoes taste a little farty when hot in this particular dish, but that's very much my own point of view.

¼ stick (25 g) butter
1 lb. (400 g) floury potatoes,
peeled and cut into rough pieces
1 leek, rinsed and roughly chopped
3 banana shallots, roughly chopped
1 clove of garlic, split
2 cups (400 ml) chicken
1 ½ cups (300 ml) heavy cream
½ cup (100 ml) whole milk
2 oz. (50 g) fresh leaf spinach
Nutmeg, grated
Salt

Melt the butter in a saucepan and add the potatoes, leeks, shallots, and garlic. Let it simmer for a few minutes and then add the broth. Boil for 5 minutes.

Pour in the cream and milk and boil until the potatoes are just done. They'll fall apart because they're floury potatoes. Blend the soup until smooth with the spinach, season with salt and a little nutmeg to taste, and let it cool completely.

Serve the soup chilled with prawns, crème fraiche and dill, or boil and serve with butter-fried leeks.

Butter-fried leeks
1 leek, finely chopped
½ stick (50 g) butter
Salt

Melt the butter in the pan. Place the leek in the pan and let it cook for a minute until soft. Season with salt to taste.

Cold potato terrine with cream cheese

I've served this terrine at family reunions, weddings, and family dinners. Basically for any celebration and god knows what else. To call it useful is an understatement. It can be served with so much and it is so popular (and you come across as a truly talented cook). Don't tell anyone how you've done it—keep it to yourself and let annoying relatives and self-proclaimed master chefs sweat a little before you reveal the method. The terrine is best with new potatoes, but it works great with waxy potatoes, too. Here's your starting point.

Once you've made the natural terrine a few times you can start to play around with seasoning. My favorites are anchovies, cold-smoked salmon, gravlax, soused herring, and bleak roe.

8–10 servings as snacks

1 lb. (400 g) small potatoes, waxy or new potatoes, scrubbed
4 cups (1 l) water
3 tsp. salt
½ bunch chives, finely chopped
½ bunch dill, finely chopped
6 gelatin leaves
2 oz. + 5 oz. (50 g + 150 g) cream cheese, e.g., Philadelphia
¾ cup (150 ml) crème fraiche

Boil the potatoes in salted water and allow to cool slightly. Cut the warm potatoes into ½ inch (1 ½ cm) pieces and mix with chives and dill.

Melt the gelatin leaves in a pan on a low heat together with 2 oz. (50 g) of cream cheese. Remove from heat and mix the gelatin and cream cheese mixture immediately with the rest of the cream cheese and crème fraiche because the gelatin hardens quickly. Fold immediately into the potato mixture.

Line a terrine mold that will hold 4 cups (1 l), or a smaller porcelain dish, with plastic foil and fill with the mixture. Fold over the plastic foil that is hanging over the edge of the mold and put under light pressure in the fridge for at least 3 hours but preferably overnight.

The terrine can be made up to 3 days in advance. When serving, first cut the terrine into slices 1 inch (3 cm) wide and then into squares.

Pitepalt

The dish that's missed the most in the home cooking book *Husman* that I published in 2016 is pitepalt, a type of meat-filled dumpling. After much deliberation, it wasn't possible to include it and I (rightly) just had to swallow it. You can't imagine how many times I've been told "Sure, the book's good, but where's pitepalt?" It's a treasure of a dish from the Norrland region of Sweden, and I truly appreciate the loyalty and pride that many people feel towards pitepalt. So it's with great pleasure that I've given it pride of place in this book about potatoes.

Pitepalt is reminiscent of Öland's kroppkakor (another kind of meat-filled dumpling, see page 70) but here only raw potatoes and barley flour are used, and the pork isn't seasoned with allspice as it is in kroppkakor. Sweetened lingonberries and butter are important accompaniments. And there's a phrase that we Swedes use to describe the feeling when we've enjoyed a hearty dinner—a *pitepalt coma*—such is the extent that we revere this dish.

1 ¾ lb. (800 g) waxy potatoes, peeled
1 cup (120 g) wheat flour
1 cup (120 g) barley flour
1 tsp. salt
5 oz. (150 g) marinated pork flank, finely diced
Sweetened lingonberries (see page 103)
Butter

Finely grate the potatoes and squeeze out as much liquid as possible from the grater. Either squeeze out the liquid with your hands or wring it out using a clean tea towel (which you don't mind getting messy).

Mix the potatoes, wheat flour, barley flour, and salt in a bowl. You may need more or less flour than the recipe calls for—the dough should be firm.

Roll balls of dough about 2 ½ inches (6 cm) in diameter. Push a small hole in the center and poke in as much pork as you dare without the dumpling cracking later. Pinch the dough together and shape into a ball again.

Boil a large pot with plenty of lightly salted water. Place each dumpling in and turn it over. Allow to simmer for about 45 to 60 minutes.

Serve the dumplings immediately or let them cool. If you let them cool, you can cut them into pieces and fry them in butter. Sweetened lingonberries and butter can be served with either option.

Following pages, left to right: Öland kroppkakor, Pitepalt, Småland kroppkakor

DESIGN

Öland kroppkakor

The eternal battle (in which the pitepalt does not participate) is over the best type of kroppkakor. Those from Öland or those from Småland. It's not a bitter feud, but it's a feud nonetheless. For me, they're two completely different dishes and therefore both must be included. I like both very much, but if someone puts a loaded gun to my head and demands to know which I prefer, it will be those from Öland. I'd rather not take sides, but that feels a bit corny.

Grated raw potatoes, slightly boiled potatoes, and wheat flour are the foundation and the key to the dough. I also like it that the pork is just diced, mixed with allspice, and not fried before being used to fill the dumplings. The pork takes on such a nice character and tastes incredible. Kroppkakor are best freshly cooked but they're also insanely good when left to cool and pan-fried. Just like with pitepalt, you may find you need more or less flour, and the dough should be firm and easy to shape into balls.

½ lb. (200 g) waxy potatoes, peeled and boiled
1 ½ lb. (600 g) waxy potatoes, peeled
½ cup (60 g) wheat flour
1 tsp. salt
5 ½ oz. (160 g) marinated pork loin, finely shredded
1 yellow onion, finely chopped
½ tsp. freshly ground allspice
Sweetened lingonberries (see page 103)
Heavy cream
Butter

Boil ½ lb. (200 g) of potatoes, then press immediately and keep warm.

Finely grate 1 ½ lb. (600 g) of potatoes and wring out the liquid thoroughly using a clean tea towel (which you don't mind getting messy).

Mix the boiled and raw potatoes, flour, and salt into a firm dough. Add more flour if necessary.

Mix the pork, onion, and allspice in a bowl.

Shape into rolls. Cut into pieces and form into balls about 2 ½ inches (6 cm) in diameter. Press a small hole into each ball and poke in a little pork and onion mixture. Pinch the dough together and shape into a ball again.

Boil a large pot with plenty of lightly salted water. Place the kroppkakor in the pan and simmer for about an hour.

Remove and serve immediately with cream, lingonberries, and butter.

Småland kroppkakor

I do like the Småland ones too, it has to be said! It's an incredible dish in its own right. The Småland kroppkakor are also much better suited for small dumplings. This really is a lovely variant, with nice little kroppkakor as big as ping-pong balls that are pan-fried until golden brown on all sides before being served.

1 ¾ lb. (800 g) waxy potatoes, peeled
1 egg
1 cup (120 g) wheat flour
½ tsp. salt
5 ½ oz. (160 g) marinated pork loin, finely shredded
1 yellow onion, finely chopped
½ tsp. freshly ground allspice
Sweetened lingonberries (see page 103)
Butter

Boil the potatoes in salted water until they're just done. Drain the water and allow the steam to evaporate quickly.

Press the potatoes immediately and mix quickly with the eggs, flour, and salt. Allow to cool slightly.

Fry the pork, onion, and allspice in butter until crispy. Drain on paper towels.

Roll the potato dough into rolls, using extra flour if needed. Cut into pieces and form into small balls.

Press a small hole into each ball and poke in a little of the pork and onion mixture. Pinch the dough together and shape into a ball again.

Boil a large pot with plenty of lightly salted water. Place the kroppkakor in the pan and simmer for about 10 minutes. The balls will float up after 6 or 7 minutes. Let them simmer on the surface for another 3 to 4 minutes.

Remove and serve immediately with lingonberries and butter.

Stewed potatoes

A lovely clear broth from cooking beef brisket, steak, or pork leg turns cloudy when potatoes and root vegetables are left to stew in it. The stewed potatoes are then served with the cooked meat when it's ready. This fabulous cooking method, beautifully simple and traditional, has given the dish its Swedish name, impotatis, which it wears with pride. The earthiness of the broth is warming and delicious with all the vegetables. Stewed potatoes are good for the stomach and they're warm and comforting.

3 cups (600 ml) broth from, e. g., brisket (see the recipe below)
3 oz. (80 g) carrots, peeled and cut into large pieces
3 oz. (80 g) celeriac, peeled and cut into large pieces
3 oz. (80 g) parsnips, roughly chopped (the peel is good, keep it)
1 yellow onion, in large pieces
1 lb. (400 g) waxy potatoes, scrubbed and cut into rough pieces

Boil the broth and add the carrots, celeriac, parsnips, and onions. Boil for 20 minutes Add the potatoes and let everything boil slowly until the potatoes are done. Remember that root vegetables that have been boiled for a short time aren't as tasty. It's better to cook the root vegetables and the potatoes a little too long.

Beef brisket

1 ¾ lb. (800 g) marinated beef brisket
1 yellow onion, roughly chopped
2 bay leaves

Rinse the beef brisket for a few minutes to remove the salt on the surface. Place the meat in a pan and fill with water so that it's well covered.

Bring to a boil, skim off what comes to the surface when boiling, and add onions and bay leaves. Cook the beef brisket for about 1 ½ hours. The time varies depending on the meat, but you should be able to use a meat fork or poke the meat when it is fully cooked without issue. Take the meat out of the broth and put it in a press while it cools.

Strain the broth and save it for the stewed potatoes. When serving, thinly slice the beef brisket and serve it together with the potatoes.

Pickled potatoes

I love to pickle vegetables. Nordic cooking has always had several elements of pickling. In preparation for our long winters, we have canned, pickled, and salted things and placed them in lactic acid. Potatoes and pickling make a great team.

They have a lovely consistency and take up the flavors really well. Here I've seasoned them with mustard seeds, but feel free to go wild with other seasonings! You can use krondill when it's in season, for example. It pairs excellently with grilled fish and smoked salmon, or try mixing a potato salad with half pickled potatoes for an extra kick. The pickling brine is cold and the potatoes go directly into it when they're steaming and freshly cooked, and allowed to cool and soak up the brine.

1 cup (200 ml) vinegar, 12 %
2 cups (340 g) granulated sugar
3 cups (600 ml) water
2 tbsp. yellow mustard seeds
1 ¾ lb. (800 g) waxy potatoes, ideally Solist, roughly 2 inches (5–6 cm) in diameter, scrubbed
2 bay leaves
2 banana shallots, sliced

Bring the vinegar, sugar, water, and mustard seeds to a boil. Allow to cool completely.

Boil the potatoes in salted water until done.

Halve the potatoes and place them still warm, interspersed with bay leaves and onions, in well-cleaned glass jars with tight-fitting lids. Pour the pickling liquid over them and seal the jars immediately. Allow to cool completely, place in the fridge, and preferably leave for a day before tasting.

The potatoes will last at least a few weeks when stored in the refrigerator.

Potato ravioli

Here it's easy to assume that some food terrorist has "Swedishized" the Italian ravioli, but let's gloss over that for now. This is a classic in parts of Italy: pasta pillows filled with potatoes are not a new invention of ours in the Nordics. You can enjoy these as they are with a little melted butter and grated Parmesan. But tomato sauce, a good ragu, or cheese sauce also works well with it. Or, as in the picture, so does a tasty, buttery broth.

Pasta dough
4 eggs
2 cups (220 g) semolina flour

Filling
½ lb. (200 g) floury potatoes
⅓ stick (30 g) butter
1 banana shallot, finely chopped
1 clove of garlic, finely grated
1 oz. (30 g) Parmesan, grated
1 bunch flat leaf parsley, coarsely chopped
Salt and freshly ground black pepper

Broth
1 banana shallot, finely chopped
1 clove of garlic, finely chopped
½ cup (100 ml) white wine
1 ½ cups (300 ml) chicken stock, diluted
⅓ stick (30 g) butter
2 oz. (50 g) Parmesan, grated
Grated zest of 1 lemon
½ bunch thyme, picked leaves
Olive oil
Salt and freshly ground black pepper

Pasta dough: Mix the eggs and flour together. A crumbly dough should form that looks like couscous. If it's too dry, add a little water. If it's too sticky, add a little flour.

Put the dough in a plastic bag and let it rest for a few hours in the fridge.

Filling: Boil the potatoes in salted water until they're just done. Mash the potatoes with a fork and let them cool a little.

Melt the butter in a pan and add the garlic and onion. Cook the mixture in the butter on a low heat for about 5 minutes. Pour over the mashed potatoes and mix well. Mix in the Parmesan and parsley and add salt and pepper to taste.

Roll out the pasta dough in a pasta machine. Dollop the filling 1 finger-width apart on half of the pasta sheet, fold over the other half, and punch out some nice ravioli.

Boil the ravioli in batches for a minute in lightly salted water. Remove with a slotted spoon.

Broth: Sauté the onion and garlic in a little olive oil in a pan for a couple of minutes without it taking color. Add the wine and let it reduce by half. Pour in the stock and boil for a few minutes. Mix or whisk in the butter and season with salt to taste. Place the freshly cooked ravioli in the broth and stir. Serve in deep dishes and top with Parmesan, lemon zest, thyme, and black pepper.

Potato aioli

There are countless ways to make aioli, but I like it best with potatoes. Any form of mayonnaise is good, but in this instance, I want a little less of that mayonnaise feeling. The potatoes add richness and creaminess to the aioli, making it perfect for fish stew or prawn fritters. I use both olive oil and canola oil. Aioli should actually only contain olive oil, but the risk is that the olive oil just overpowers the overall flavor, so I use fifty-fifty olive oil and canola oil.

Approx. 4 oz. (100 g) floury potatoes, peeled
2 tsp. Dijon mustard
2 egg yolks
Juice of ½ lemon
2 garlic cloves, grated
½ cup (100 ml) olive oil
½ cup (100 ml) canola oil
Salt and freshly ground black pepper

Boil the potatoes just until ready in salted water and allow to cool slightly.

Mash the potatoes with a fork in a bowl.

Mix in the mustard, egg yolks, lemon juice, and garlic. Whisk in the oils in a thin stream and season with salt, pepper, and more lemon juice if needed. If the aioli becomes too thick, dilute it with a little cold water.

Baked

When potatoes are cooked in the oven, we get a different type of product than when they're boiled. The main difference compared with boiling or frying is that the sweet flavors come through, regardless of which recipe you're using. This is because the cooking sort of pushes the sugars out when there's no water or frying oil involved. You could be forgiven for thinking that there shouldn't be that big of a difference between oven-roasted and fried potatoes, but it's mainly the sweetness and the round flavor that make the difference.

The oven is the most convenient cooking method.
The food takes care of itself and you don't have to constantly keep an eye on it. Peace and quiet can prevail in the kitchen.

Potato wedges

You can easily cobble this together in a few seconds when inspiration strikes. That's the best way to sum up potato wedges. It may sound dull, but it's true! It's a quick and universal potato dish to turn to in many situations in our tightly planned lives. Potato wedges are waxy, raw potatoes cut into wedges that are then roasted in the oven. The fact that the wedges are raw when they're put in the oven makes it a little difficult to get them super crispy, but it also means that you get a sweet and tasty potato with a lovely oven-roasted feel. Not everything has to be crispy. We'll get to that killer crispiness further on, but for now we'll settle for ordinary but damn good potato wedges.

I have my own version to lift the humble potato wedge up a notch. It comes in the form of a dressing that the wedges are enrobed in when they come piping hot out of the oven. This is what lifts them from superstar to messiah. The trick with this quick potato dish is that you just have to run wild with the seasoning.

1 ¾ lb. (800 g) waxy potatoes, ideally Amandine, scrubbed and halved
Olive oil
Salt

Dressing
2 banana shallots, finely chopped
1 clove of garlic, finely chopped
Grated zest of 1 lemon
1 red chili, seeded and finely chopped
1 tbsp. thyme or rosemary (preferably fresh, but dried also works)
¼ cup (50 ml) olive oil

Set the oven to 430 °F (220 °C) fan.

Dressing: Mix the shallots, garlic, lemon zest, chili, herbs, and olive oil. Set aside until it's time to serve.

Roll the potato wedges around on a plate of olive oil and salt.

Roast in the middle of the oven for about 30 minutes, turning a couple of times in the process.

When the potatoes come out of the oven, mix them in with the dressing and serve immediately on a plate.

Potato wedges are a friend of many different dishes, but grilled in the summer is probably number one. Right?

Pressed potatoes—my ultimate roast potato

No more nonsense with dowdy potato wedges. (I do love potato wedges, but let's pick up the pace a little.) I'm going to tell you about my best oven-roasted potatoes—pre-cooked and lightly pressed potatoes, roasted to perfection. Floury potatoes are the order of the day here, and the secret is to boil them and break them a little at the edges when you press them with a fork directly on the plate. Just a light press and then add some olive oil, browned butter, and salt before sliding the tray into the oven. It doesn't matter if the potato falls into pieces, this isn't a beauty contest. The crumbs and more intact pieces all end up in the same bowl when serving, and it's those crumbs that are the tastiest!

I usually eat pressed potatoes instead of fries with fried fish and curry remoulade. But they're also good for stews, grilled, or on their own dipped in mayo. You can then experiment a little with the flavors for the butter that you drizzle over the potatoes. Toss with herbs and olives perhaps? We've tried chive butter, too. Delicious!

1 ¾ lb. (800 g) floury potatoes, roughly 3 inches (7–8 cm) in diameter, scrubbed
3 tsp. salt
¼ cup (50 ml) olive oil
¾ stick (75 g) butter, browned
1 clove of garlic, mashed with a knife
½ bunch thyme

Set the oven to 400 °F (200 °C) fan.

Boil the potatoes in salted water until they just start to cook and break a little at the edges. Drain the water and allow the steam to quickly evaporate from the potatoes.

Scoop out the potatoes onto a greased tray and press each potato a little with a fork. They should be broken but still hold together.

Season with salt and drizzle with olive oil and browned butter. Put the garlic and thyme sprigs on top of the potatoes.

Roast hot in the middle of the oven for about 20 minutes or until the potatoes are really golden brown and super crispy. For extra color and crispness, turn on the broiler for the last 5 minutes.

Remove the potatoes and place them in a bowl. Get all the broken bits as well, drizzle with some of the fat from the pan, and season with salt.

Hasselback potatoes

The mother of all roast potatoes and the ruler of the potato world. The Hasselback potato dictates the terms and is the inspirer, always dependable, and always the best. In my world, this is the perfected end product. I like that it's a roast potato. It doesn't have to be super crispy all the way through. It's good even when it's just a little crunchy here and there on top. As you work your way inwards to where the butter and salt have run into the slits, each potato becomes a delight. I've actually changed my mind on the Hasselback issue. In the past, I always did without the breadcrumbs, but I've slowly changed my position and have reached the conclusion that I like it with breadcrumbs. They actually make it better.

The essence of my life is now Hasselback potatoes. I make a deep-fried version at the restaurant and serve it as a snack with bleak roe and sour cream. But that's a completely different matter that I'll come back to on page 168. I've scored so many Hasselback potatoes in my life, both at home and in restaurants. I can quite categorically say that no one has ever scored more Hasselback potatoes than I have ... millions of scores.

¼ cup (40 g) breadcrumbs
½ stick (50 g) butter, cold from the refrigerator
1 ¾ lb. (800 g) waxy potatoes, roughly 3 inches (7–8 cm) in diameter, scrubbed
Salt and freshly ground black pepper

Set the oven to 400 °F (200 °C) fan.

Slice the potatoes finely but not all the way through. Place them in an ovenproof dish, season with salt and pepper, and sprinkle with the breadcrumbs. Grate the butter over them with a cheese grater so that it covers the potatoes.

Bake in the middle of the oven for 40 to 50 minutes or until the potatoes are really baked through, crispy on top, and golden brown.

The absolute flagship of Sunday dinner, both with steak and grilled chicken. It also works great with vegetarian dishes!

Pommes Anna

Thinly sliced potatoes tossed with melted butter, garlic, herbs, and salt before being baked straight in a mold, much like potato gratin but without the cream and milk. I have my own way of making Pommes Anna. In order to get a nice crisp on as much of the potato as possible, I place the slices upright and tightly together and bake them. The effect is similar to Hasselback potatoes with lots of tasty, crispy slices. You have to be able to change up the classics from time to time. Feel free to make Pommes Anna with small potatoes. Although it's a bit of a pain, it's worth all the effort. I brown the melted butter for even more flavor, and all the sludge that collects at the bottom of the pan when the butter is browned goes with it. Some people think that Pommes Anna is a type of terrine that you cut into slices, but that's not quite true. In fact, a potato terrine is something completely different.

Pommes Anna is a perfect showpiece to put on the table with roast lamb with garlic and rosemary, or with a good vegetarian bean stew.

1 ¾ lb. (800 g) waxy potatoes, scrubbed
1 stick (100 g) butter, browned
2 garlic cloves, grated
½ bunch rosemary, picked and finely chopped leaves
½ bunch thyme, ripped leaves
Salt
Canola oil for the mold

Set the oven to 400 °F (200 °C) fan.

Cut the potatoes into very thin slices (about ⅛ inch/2 mm) and place them in a bowl. Add butter, garlic, rosemary, thyme, and salt and turn the slices around in the mixture.

Grease a round mold, about 8 inches (20 cm) in diameter, with oil. Place the potato slices upright all the way around the mold. Start at the outer edge and continue layer by layer all the way to the center of the mold. Try to pack the slices as tightly as possible.

Brush a little extra butter on the top and bake in the middle of the oven for 40 to 50 minutes or until the potatoes are golden brown and crispy.

Potato rose

This is a take on Pommes Anna, but it's more elegant and comes in single-serve portions. There are countless variations of the potato rose. It's just a case of flavoring the butter or making a thin sauce and dipping the potato slices in it before putting them in the molds. I've come up with a sage butter, dill butter, and horseradish butter. And I've styled it with tomato sauce, a thin cheese sauce, and various herb sauces. All of them have worked perfectly and left me really impressed. Just follow the technique and stick to the basic recipe before letting your imagination run wild. It's a little tricky and requires some equipment, but really it's just time and patience that are the order of the day here.

1 ¾ lb. (800 g) waxy potatoes, scrubbed
1 stick (100 g) butter, melted
1 clove of garlic, peeled
Salt

Set the oven to 350 °F (180 °C) fan.

Cook the garlic clove in the butter on a low heat for 10 minutes. Remove the clove of garlic.

Slice the potatoes into very thin slices (about about ⅛ inch/2 mm) and coat them in the butter. Salt them well.

Line a muffin pan with greaseproof paper in each individual muffin mold. Cover the bottom with a few slices of potato and then arrange the slices around the outside and right up to the edge. Continue inward until a nice rose has formed.

Bake in the middle of the oven for 50 minutes, until the potatoes are baked through, have a nice color, and are a little crunchy. Remove the roses from the molds and serve immediately. You can also make the roses in advance and heat them up before serving.

Baked potatoes

The beauty here is that the potatoes are simply baked in the oven, without any seasoning or anything else to get in the way. Not even salt. Just potatoes, from start to finish. Then—when you have baked, cut, and pressed the potatoes—you can add all kinds of flavorings.

My approach? Keep it simple. The best things (as so often) are butter and salt. But of course, a good mix of other things couldn't hurt, right? When it comes to fillings, I have a real killer: sikaforsröra with smoked reindeer steak, horseradish, and roe. Skagen mix and other mixes, such as salmon, are too airy here. Sikaforsröra in all its glory is what you need here.

Baked potatoes also work superbly as an accompaniment to a variety of dishes. Just spoon out the potatoes for pure enjoyment. Another good tip is actually to try eating it as it is, in its most naked guise, without any disturbance. Not even salt.

4 baking potatoes, roughly 3 inches (7–8 cm) in diameter, scrubbed

Set the oven to 435 °F (225 °C) fan.

Place the potatoes on a baking sheet and bake for about 50 to 60 minutes in the middle of the oven.

Remove from the oven, cut a cross in the middle of each potato and press down. Serve immediately.

Sikafors mix

8 oz. (200 g) smoked reindeer steak, finely diced
3 scallions, finely sliced
2 tsp. horseradish paste
¼ cup (50 ml) mayonnaise
¼ cup (50 ml) crème fraiche
4 oz. (100 g) whitefish roe or bleak roe
1 pc. fresh horseradish to garnish
Salt and freshly ground black pepper

Mix the reindeer steak, scallions, horseradish paste, mayonnaise, and crème fraiche. Season with salt and pepper to taste.

Cross the potato through the middle and press it so that it opens. Fill with the sikaforsröra, top with roe, and grate horseradish on top. There'll be some of the mixture, roe, and horseradish left over, so add more while you eat.

Following pages: Parmesan potatoes and Dirty potatoes.

Parmesan potatoes

The umami scale (if there were such a thing) would hit the roof if you were measuring Parmesan. Our mouth curls with pleasure and the flavors reach our ears. I couldn't go a day in the kitchen without Parmesan.

Here, I scrub and halve the potatoes before cooking them with salt and a bit of bicarbonate of soda—this raises the pH and breaks down the surface of the potatoes, making them crispier. I then roll the potatoes in butter, lemon zest, and Parmesan and roast them in a hot oven. When Parmesan is roasted, turns golden brown, and is allowed to cool just a little, it becomes incredibly crunchy and the umami flavor develops even more. But be careful not to get let it get too much color, because burnt Parmesan just isn't good.

1 ¾ lb. (800 g) waxy potatoes, roughly 3 inches (7–8 cm) in diameter, scrubbed and halved
4 cups (1 l) water
3 tsp. salt
1 tbsp. baking soda
½ stick (50 g) butter, melted
4 oz. (100 g) Parmesan, finely grated
Finely grated zest of 1 lemon
1 bunch thyme, picked leaves

Measure the water and salt into a pot. Add the potatoes and bring to a boil. Add the bicarbonate of soda, lower the heat, and simmer for around 20 minutes. Drain the water, let the steam evaporate, and allow to cool almost completely.

Set the oven to 400 °F (200 °C) fan.

Roll the potatoes around in the butter, Parmesan, lemon zest, and thyme. Spread the potatoes out on a baking sheet and roast in the middle of the oven for around 25 minutes. Try to make sure that the potatoes aren't placed too close together.

Turn occasionally and continue roasting until the potatoes are golden brown and crispy.

Dirty potatoes

When I worked at Hotel Borgholm, many years ago, Karin Fransson taught me to make dirty potatoes. The first thing you react to is the name—dirty potatoes?! Typical of Karin to come up with such a name and such a way of serving them! My recipe is a little different from Karin's, but all credit for this dish goes to her. The potatoes are sinful, roasted first before being dressed in tapenade and herbs and then left to roast for a few more minutes in the oven. It's a real umami bomb! I remember that we had dirty potatoes on the menu in the restaurant and that later in the evening they were ordered as snacks in the bar. I can tell you that the dish was equally popular as a snack and as a main meal.

At home I eat dirty potatoes as they are, with vegetables and a cold sauce. But they also work with herb-baked salmon in the oven or as a side dish for seafood.

1 ¾ lb. (800 g) waxy potatoes, ideally Ratte or asparagus potato, roughly 3 inches (7–8 cm) in diameter, unpeeled
3 tbsp. olive oil
½ bunch thyme, picked leaves
½ bunch oregano, picked leaves

Tapenade

1 ½ cups (135 g) black pitted olives, coarsely chopped
4 anchovy fillets
2 tbsp. capers
2 garlic cloves, grated
¾ cup (150 ml) olive oil
2 tbsp. squeezed lemon juice
Salt

Set the oven to 430 °F (220 °C) fan.

Tapenade: Add the olives, anchovies, capers, garlic, olive oil, and lemon juice in a blender. Blend for a minute or so until you have a fairly smooth tapenade. Set aside until the potatoes are ready.

Put the potatoes on a plate and coat with olive oil. Roast in the middle of the oven for about 30 minutes. Remove and coat in the tapenade and herbs, then put back in the oven and roast for another 5 minutes. Give them a stir halfway through, place on a platter, and serve immediately.

Potato fondant

I don't know where the word fondant comes from. Fondant means that something is viscous, like a chocolate fondant. But this is about potatoes, and we all know they're not viscous! A similarity could be that chocolate fondant is usually packed with fat and here we're also talking about an ingredient baked in butter and a little olive oil.

There are any number of variations on potato fondant. Some people add a little stock as well, but I go with just butter and oil to get a really rich fondant. Like so many times already in this book, I brown the butter, let it cool a bit, and add the potatoes, pressing in the herbs and garlic. The butter and oil absorb the flavors incredibly well and transport them into the potatoes.

I always bake with quite a lot of pearl onions for the sake of taste, but also because the onions go incredibly well together with the potatoes and what you serve them with.

1 ¾ lb. (800 g) waxy potatoes, roughly 3 inches (7–8 cm) in diameter, scrubbed and halved
Salt
⅓ stick (30 g) butter
16 pearl onions (frying onions)
4 ½ sticks (500 g) butter, browned
½ cup (100 ml) olive oil
1 bunch thyme
1 bunch rosemary
3 cloves of garlic, peeled

Set the oven to 300 °F (150 °C) no fan.

Brown the potato halves in ⅓ stick (30 g) of butter in a frying pan, on all sides but mainly on the cut surface.

Place the potatoes and onions in an ovenproof dish, season with salt, and coat evenly.

Pour over the browned butter that has cooled a little and olive oil to cover the potatoes. Distribute thyme and rosemary sprigs in the dish, including the stems. Add garlic.

Bake in the middle of the oven for about an hour until the potatoes are really soft all the way through. Allow to cool slightly.

Remove the herbs and garlic first, then the potatoes and onions, and serve.

They go really well with grilled chicken or a grilled piece of meat.

Salmon pudding

For me, salmon pudding is a clear potato dish. It's out of this world, and simply one of the best. Be careful when making salmon pudding. Take your time and appreciate the fiddling and tinkering. This will all pay off in the form of a lovely salmon pudding that's worthy of a Michelin star. Make sure to cook lots of onions in butter and spoon over plenty of the egg mixture so it ends up all around and between each layer. And make sure you have plenty of salmon! A potato dish it may be, but it's also a salmon pudding. Follow the recipe and get a black belt in fiddly cooking.

1 ¾ lb. (800 g) waxy potatoes, peeled and boiled
½ stick (50 g) butter
2 yellow onions, finely sliced
3 eggs
¾ cup (150 ml) heavy cream
Finely grated zest of 1 lemon
17 oz. (480 g) marinated salmon (see page 42), in approx. ½-inch (1-cm) thick slices
1 bunch dill, roughly chopped
1 lemon, in wedges
5 oz. (140 g) clarified butter, for serving
Salt and freshly ground black pepper

Set the oven to 350 °F (175 °C) fan.

Slice the potatoes into slices ¼-inch (½-cm) thick.

Melt ½ stick (50 g) of butter in a saucepan, add the onion, and cook for a few minutes until soft. Strain off the butter and let the onion cool.

Whisk the eggs and cream together. Season with salt and pepper and add the lemon zest.

Now all the ingredients are ready for assembly: Start by lining an ovenproof dish (roughly 9 ½ inches or 24 cm in diameter) with an even layer of potatoes. Spoon over some of the egg mixture, cover with salmon slices, and spoon over additional egg mixture. Press lightly with your hand to make the pudding compact. Then add a layer of onion, some egg mixture, dill, and finally a layer of potatoes in a nice pattern on the top. Press down with your hand to make the pudding really compact and spoon over the rest of the egg mixture.

Bake in the middle of the oven for around an hour. Serve with lemon wedges and clarified butter.

Lufsa

Lufsa is a dish from Öland made from grated potatoes and roast pork. It's home cooking at its best, not least because it's a great one-pot meal, yet unfortunately it gets overshadowed by Öland's other famous potato dish, kroppkakor (see page 70). And so I have to come to the rescue. One of the first recipes I wrote for this book was actually lufsa. That's how much I like this all-in-one dish. Finely grate the potatoes and wring them out in a towel. You need all the liquid out to achieve perfection in this dish. So do it properly—half the secret of this recipe is getting the liquid out.

1 lb. (400 g) marinated roast pork, sliced
1 ¾ lb. (800 g) waxy potatoes, scrubbed
2 eggs
1 ½ cups (300 ml) heavy cream
½ cup (60 g) wheat flour
Butter
Salt

Set the oven to 400 °F (200 °C) fan. Fry the pork quite well in a dry frying pan. Strain off the fat and save it. Drain the pork on paper towels.

Grate the potatoes finely and lightly salt them. Place the gratings in a clean kitchen towel that you're not worried about getting messy and wring out as much liquid as possible.

Mix the eggs, cream, flour, salt, and saved fat in a bowl. Fold the potatoes into the batter.

Line a greased ovenproof dish (about 9 ½ inches or 24 cm in diameter) with half of the pork, pour over the potato batter, and top with the rest of the pork.

Bake in the middle of the oven for around 40 minutes. Serve with sweetened lingonberries.

Sweetened lingonberries
2 ½ cups (500 g) lingonberries
1 ¼ cup (250 g) granulated sugar

Gently stir the lingonberries and sugar together in a bowl. Cover the bowl in plastic and let it stand at room temperature for a few hours. Stir occasionally so that the sugar dissolves.

Potato roll

Actually, this recipe might be a bit too advanced to include, but it's part of my cooking history so I want to include it anyway. It's my own invention (I came up with the recipe when I was grating potatoes for Öland kroppkakor) and it has competed in Chef of the Year and figured in dishes at the restaurant. It may be a little too much, but if any daredevils want to give it a try, I'd be more than happy. Since this method is a little easier to get to grips with and can also be made a little coarser, this is the one I'm sharing here. I've made a filling with mushrooms, but once you've mastered the technique, you can play around with the fillings to your heart's content.

1½ lb. (600 g) waxy potatoes, peeled
3 eggs
Salt and freshly ground black pepper

Mushroom filling

14 oz. (400 g) mushrooms, e. g., shiitake, button mushrooms, or chanterelles, in rough pieces
Canola oil
½ stick (50 g) butter
1 banana shallot, sliced
Parmesan
Salt and freshly ground black pepper

Set the oven to 300 °F (150 °C) fan.

Finely grate the potatoes and place the gratings on a clean kitchen towel that you're not too worried about getting messy. Salt the potatoes and wring out the liquid well using the towel.

Place the grated potato in a bowl. Add the eggs and coat well, and season with pepper. Spread out the batter in a ¼-inch (½-cm) thick layer on a sheet with baking paper. Bake in the middle of the oven for 15 minutes.

Remove the potato cake, turn it out on a cutting board so that the baking paper ends up on top and carefully pull off the paper, like when you pull off the paper from a thin sponge cake base for a Swiss roll. Cut the cake into 4 rectangles.

Mushroom filling: Fry the mushrooms in oil on a high heat until all the liquid that forms in the pan has evaporated.

Add butter and onion and fry until everything has a nice color. Season with salt and pepper to taste. Pour onto a plate lined with paper towels, drain, and cool completely.

Increase the oven to 430 °F (220 °C) fan.

Spread the mushroom filling on the potato rectangles. Roll up and put on a new baking sheet lined with baking paper. Sprinkle generously with Parmesan and gratinate for about 10 minutes.

Potato terrine

Now we're really in the restaurant kitchen and clattering about. For me, potato terrine is thinly sliced potatoes baked in the oven to perfection. After baking, the terrine is pressed to even greater perfection and then cut to a millimeter's precision. There are a multitude of different ways to make potato terrine, but for me it's thinly sliced potatoes that are salted, tossed in butter, and sprinkled with grated cheese in the mold before being baked. Cheese is a good (the best) partner for potatoes, and here Västerbotten cheese contributes to the depth of the overall flavor and the creamy texture in the middle.

1 ¾ lb. (800 g) floury potatoes, scrubbed
2 banana shallots, thinly sliced
1 stick (100 g) butter
5 oz. (150 g) Västerbotten cheese or other mature cheese, grated
Salt
Butter for frying

Set the oven to 300 °F (150 °C) fan.

Slice the potatoes into very thin (⅛ inch / 2 mm) slices using a mandolin.

Cook the onion in the butter for around 10 minutes on a medium heat until soft. Use a pan that's large enough to accommodate the potatoes as well. Coat the potatoes in the onion mixture and salt well.

Layer the potatoes and cheese in a terrine or loaf pan lined with baking paper. The pan should be around 50 fl. oz. (1 ½ l) in size. Finish with a layer of potato. Fold over the baking paper once the terrine is fully assembled and bake in the middle of the oven for about an hour.

Put the terrine in a press, first at room temperature and then in the refrigerator. For example, you can fill a mold with water and place it on the terrine or take something else heavy like a cast iron mortar.

When serving, slice the terrine into fine slices and fry them in butter until crispy.

Dried potatoes

This sounds insanely advanced and it's almost a bit of a lab warning for dried potatoes, but it sounds and looks a lot more advanced than it actually is. As with many of the basic recipes in this book, you can take this as far as you like. Once you've mastered the basic recipe, dried potatoes can come in many shapes and forms. Actually, it works by simply boiling potatoes, squeezing them, spreading them out on a silicone mat, and drying them in the oven. I spice things up with egg whites to make the crispiness extra stable.

Use dried potatoes as a garnish for various dishes or break them into pieces and dip them in tasty dips and use as an aperitif snack—just do something with them! And if you don't want to do anything with them right away, they can be stored in an airtight container with a lid for at least a week at room temperature.

1 ¾ lb. (800 g) waxy or floury potatoes, roughly 3 inches (7–8 cm) in diameter, peeled
4 cups (1 l) water
3 tsp. salt
3 egg whites

Measure the water and salt into a pot. Add the potatoes and bring to a boil. Lower the heat and simmer in gently bubbling water for about 20 minutes. Drain the water and allow the steam to evaporate from the potatoes for a minute.

Set the oven to 200 °F (90 °C) no fan.

Press the potato and mix it with the egg whites. Spread the mixture thinly (about ⅛-inch, 2-mm thick) on a silicone mat and dry in the middle of the oven for about 2 hours. Take out and leave to cool.

When serving, break into the size of pieces you want.

Potato focaccia from Puglia

Bread has always been baked with potatoes, especially in years of need when there was a shortage of grain and potatoes were used to make the bread more nutritious. But you gain in moistness, shelf-life, and taste. I've baked many different kinds of potato bread and I've now arrived at the potato focaccia, my absolute favorite potato bread. I love focaccia even without potato—it's an incredible bread in every way. It's easy to bake (suits me), moist (suits me), useful (also suits me), and incredibly tasty (suits me especially well). Potato focaccia is baked in Puglia in southern Italy and is also called focaccia pugliese. You just have to love that last piece of the puzzle—the name.

¾ lb. (300 g) waxy or floury potatoes, roughly 3 inches (7–8 cm) in diameter, peeled
2 ½ cups (500 ml) water for the potatoes
1 ½ tsp. salt for the potatoes
¾ oz. (20 g) yeast
1 ¼ cup (250 ml) lukewarm water
½ cup (100 ml) olive oil
1 ½ tsp. salt
14 oz. (400 g) wheat flour
8 small potatoes, finely sliced
Salt flakes
½ bunch rosemary
¼ cup (50 ml) olive oil for the mold

Measure the water and salt into a pot. Add ¾ lb. (300 g) of potatoes and bring to a boil. Lower the heat and simmer in gently bubbling water for about 20 minutes. Drain the water and allow the steam to evaporate for a minute. Press the potatoes and let them cool to room temperature.

Dissolve the yeast in the warm water and add the pressed potatoes, ½ cup (100 ml) of olive oil, salt, and a little of the flour until the dough comes together. Add the rest of the flour and continue kneading the dough in the machine for 15 minutes. If you make the dough by hand, "knead" it in a bowl using a wooden spoon. Then let the dough rise for 40 minutes at room temperature under a baking sheet.

Set the oven to 435 °F (225 °C) no fan.

Line a round mold, about 8 ½ inches (22 cm) in diameter, with baking paper and pour the dough into the mold. Press out the dough to the edges, cover with a baking sheet, and leave for another 30 minutes.

Press holes into the dough using your fingers. Mix ¼ cup (50 ml) of olive oil and 3 tbsp. of water and brush the surface of the dough liberally with the mixture. Add the sliced potatoes and sprinkle generously with salt flakes and rosemary.

Bake in the middle of the oven for around 35 minutes. Turn onto a wire rack and let it cool slightly before serving. The bread will last for several days.

Crown cake

As a cook in the navy, I often had to whip up a crown cake while seasick and on shaky legs. I've no idea if it was invented by someone from the military or if it has some special connection, but we always made it with pride. It first appeared in 1903 in the first edition of Hemmets kokbok for home cooking. When we were ordered to make this potato-based almond cake, we served it with coffee or as a dessert. The cake is baked completely without flour, which gives it a special character. The potato could make it heavy, but the lemon and almond keep the flag flying. I like unblanched almonds, and I don't think you should blanch and peel them. The husk of the almond adds character when it's ground in an almond mill. Don't blend them in a blender—get yourself an almond mill. It'll change your life.
I brown the butter and that's my gift to this cake, which in the original "only" has melted butter. With the browned butter and the husk left on the almond, we're approaching world-class territory! A good jam and lightly whipped cream are mandatory.

1 cake

½ lb. (250 g) waxy or floury potatoes, peeled
2 ½ cups (500 ml) water
1 ½ tsp. salt
8 oz. (200 g) granulated sugar
3 eggs
1 stick (100 g) butter, lightly browned
5 oz. (150 g) sweet almonds, ground
2 bitter almonds, finely grated
Zest of ½ lemon, grated

Set the oven to 350 °F (175 °C) no fan.

Measure the water and salt into a pot. Add the potatoes and bring to a boil. Lower the heat and simmer in gently bubbling water for about 20 minutes, until the potatoes are ready. Drain the water and allow the steam to evaporate for a minute. Press the potatoes and let them cool to room temperature.

Whisk the sugar and eggs until fluffy.

Mix in the butter, almonds, bitter almonds, potatoes, and lemon zest. Pour the batter into a greased mold, about 8 inches (20 cm) in diameter, and bake in the middle of the oven for about 35 minutes. Use a skewer to test when the cake is ready.

Let the cake stand and cool to room temperature before eating it with jam and whipped cream.

Potato pizza

You're kidding?! Everything I like in one dish. Potatoes and pizza. If, god forbid, I had to get rid of all the fast food and could keep only one thing, it would be pizza (if it really counts fast food, but now we're saying it). Any kind of pizza is good—Neapolitan, Roman, Chicago style, and homemade. And with potatoes, you're onto a real winner.

Onions are also important on this pizza, which really "only" consists of a nice dough, crème fraiche, cheese, lightly boiled and sliced potatoes, and then onions. Hard rock pizza!

The dough takes a few hours. I'm definitely not a pizza perfectionist, but you can spend a little time on your pizza. It works fine to bake pizza at full pelt in your home oven. If so, pre-heat the oven with a pizza stone, and then turn on the broiler just before the pizza goes in.

Now, I'm only using potatoes and onions as a topping here, but when I feel extra greedy, I dice pancetta or bacon which I sprinkle on top before baking.

Dough

12 oz. (340 ml) water
⅛ oz. (3 g) yeast
2 tsp. salt
1 ½ lb. (600 g) wheat flour, preferably extra strong type tipo 00
1 ½ oz. (40 g) canola oil

Topping

1 lb. (400 g) floury potatoes, scrubbed
2 banana shallots, sliced
1 clove of garlic, finely sliced
Olive oil
1 cup (200 ml) crème fraiche
2 oz. (60 g) mature cheese
Salt flakes
½ bunch rosemary

Dough: Mix water and yeast in a bowl, making sure the yeast dissolves properly. Mix in salt and flour and fold in the oil in the yeast mixture. Once all the flour has been added, knead for 10 minutes by hand (or 5 minutes in a machine with a dough hook). Bring the dough together into a nice ball and let it rest on a floured counter for 10 minutes, covered with an upside-down bowl.

Divide the dough into 4 pieces, roll into nice balls, and place them in a mold.

Cover the mold with plastic wrap. Leave for at least 4 hours in the refrigerator. (The dough can rest in the refrigerator for up to 2 days before baking.)

Remove the dough balls from the refrigerator a couple of hours before baking so they come to room temperature.

Topping: Set the oven to its maximum temperature, on fan.

Slice the potatoes super thin and put them in ice water.

Soften the onion and garlic in olive oil for a few minutes, add a little salt and leave to cool.

Make one pizza at a time. Form a round pizza base by rolling a ball of dough fairly thin straight onto a floured pizza peel. Top with the crème fraiche, cheese, onion, and potatoes. Sprinkle with salt flakes, a few rosemary leaves, and finally drizzle a little olive oil on top. Bake in the oven on maximum heat, preferably on a pizza stone. Keep an eye on the time. If you've really got the heat going, it'll be done in a few minutes. Take the pizza out, place directly on a plate, and drizzle with a little extra olive oil.

Gratins

Many people's favorite among potatoes is the potato gratin. It's incredibly tasty and gratifying to make when you have guests or just for your nearest and dearest.

But there are other insanely good gratins to sink your teeth into as well, and to qualify among the gratins in this book, the yardstick is that it must be a form of all-in-one cooking and that the creation itself must (of course) be gratinated. You mix a lot of tasty things in with potatoes, put it into a mold, and bake in the oven until done and the top is gratinated. Them's the rules! The beauty of this is that you can make up your own gratins from what you have in the fridge, much like a midnight sandwich.

Potato gratin

At least, that's what most people think when it comes to gratin and potatoes. Everyone has their own way of making the "best potato gratin." The fact that ready-made potato gratins in a vacuum bag have crept in to "make life easier" is, however, more difficult to understand than for other ready-made dishes, because it's so easy to make yourself. Of course, time is the culprit in the drama. But do it my way and boil the sliced potatoes in the creamed milk before gratinating, and it will go (almost) as fast as buying pre-made!

It's important to slice the potatoes thinly. The gratin will be tastier and the texture will be much better than if you have thick slices. That's why I use waxy potatoes that hold up well even in thin slices. Some people like to use floury potatoes, but then my whole idea of the potato gratin falls flat.

½ stick (50 g) butter
3 yellow onions, finely sliced
1 ¼ cup (250 ml) heavy cream
½ cup (100 ml) whole milk
½ clove of garlic, finely grated
Salt and freshly ground black pepper
1 ¾ lb. (800 g) waxy potatoes, peeled and finely sliced
1 cup (80 g) grated mature cheese

Set the oven to 350 °F (175 °C) fan.

Sauté the onion in the butter, pour in the cream, milk, garlic, salt, and pepper. Bring to a boil. Taste whether more salt and pepper are needed.

Add the potatoes, bring to a boil, and allow to boil for a few minutes. Stir constantly with a wooden spoon so it doesn't burn on the bottom.

Pour the potatoes into a greased baking dish. Sprinkle over the cheese and finish baking the gratin in the middle of the oven for 30 to 40 minutes.

So, what about this thing about potato gratin being tastier the next day?

Always make too much! That's just one of the rules of life.

Finnish potato casserole

I love Finland and I love casseroles, one of Finland's finest imprints on the world of food. These casseroles made from, for example, turnips, carrots, or potatoes are so strong and traditional in their own rough way that you'll fall head over heels for them. Finland adores its casseroles and so do I. The important thing about the potato casserole is that when the potatoes are cooked and mixed with wheat flour, they have to be left to stand for a few hours so that the sweetness in the potatoes can develop and add flavor. So don't be stingy with the time!

The casserole is a Christmas staple in Finland, but it's also perfect as an accompaniment to things like sausages or grilled fish, or as a vegetarian dish. I just have to include a recipe for Finnish carrot casserole, too, which I love. The carrots can be replaced with turnips and then you have the classic of classics when it comes to casseroles.

1 ¾ lb. (800 g) waxy potatoes, peeled
4 tbsp. wheat flour
2 tbsp. + 1 tbsp. butter
1 ½ cups (300 ml) whole milk
2 tbsp. breadcrumbs
Salt

Boil the potatoes without salt just until done and use a fork to mash them with the flour and 2 tbsp. of butter. Leave to stand for 2 hours.

Set the oven to 350 °F (175 °C) fan.

Mix the milk into the potatoes and season with salt. Distribute in a greased baking dish, spread over the rest of the butter, and sprinkle with breadcrumbs. Bake in the middle of the oven for 45 minutes until the color is a nice golden brown.

Carrot casserole
18 oz. (500 g) carrots, peeled and cut into rough pieces
¼ cup (50 ml) whole milk
1 ½ tbsp. (25 g) semolina
¼ stick (25 g) butter
Salt and freshly ground white pepper

Set the oven to 400 °F (200 °C).

Boil the carrots until soft in salted water and mash them with a fork.

Mix the milk and semolina in a bowl and leave to swell for about 30 minutes. Mix the carrots in with the semolina mixture and add salt and pepper to taste.

Grease an ovenproof dish and pour in the carrot batter. Spread over the butter and bake in the middle of the oven for about 30 minutes.

Jansson's Temptation

This is the ultimate classic in Swedish home cooking, to the point of being a national dish. It came about after an upper-class woman in Östermalm watched the film *Jansson's Temptation* and became so enamored with the lead actor, Jansson, played by the super hunk of the time, Edvin Adolphson. She marched straight home to her housekeeper and demanded a dish named after the film. The cook made a sandwich with potatoes and anchovies and so *Jansson's Temptation* was born. How it was then transformed into one of the best potato dishes of all time is shrouded in mystery, but surely everyone agrees that this is one of the finest dishes Sweden has?

Unfortunately, Jansson is almost always misplaced at the warm end of the Christmas buffet table, when its correct location is by the herring. And maybe Jansson is also a little upset about being forced to be part of every single celebration in Sweden, but that's just the cross he has to bear. Being so loved comes at a cost!

½ stick (50 g) butter
2 yellow onions, finely sliced
1 ¾ lb. (800 g) waxy potatoes, peeled and shredded
4 ½ oz. (125 g) anchovies + liquid
2 cups (400 ml) heavy cream
1 tbsp. unsmoked caviar, e. g. Ejderns (if desired)
Breadcrumbs
Anchovies to garnish (if desired)
Butter
Salt

Set the oven to 400 °F (200 °C) fan. Sauté the onion until soft in the butter. Line the bottom of a greased ovenproof dish with half of the potatoes. Lightly salt, lay out the anchovies (save the brine) in fine rows on the potatoes, continue with the onions and finally with a layer of potatoes. Lightly salt.

Mix the cream and caviar in a bowl. Pour the anchovy brine over the gratin and then the cream. Press the potatoes so that you get a glimpse of the cream. Sprinkle with breadcrumbs, blob the butter on, and bake in the middle of the oven for about an hour.

Tartiflette

Potato gratin with pork and Reblochon cheese. French romanticism at the highest level! Once I came through France on my way down to Europe—this was before the days of GPS and computers. I had a paper map and we were to make our way from the incredible town of Clermont-Ferrand (which incidentally is very close to Puy, where the incredible lentils are grown, but that's a whole other book). After our visit, we were to go down toward Spain and in the afternoon we went toward what we thought was an open road to the south. It was spring, and that evening we ended up in a mountain massif in the middle of a snowstorm with only fumes left in the gas tank.

Confused, we recognized place names on the map, but we saw no houses, let alone a gas station. It started to get late, even more snow came down, and we were stressed, tired, and hungry. We came to what could be called a mountain village. We finally got some gas in the tank before stumbling, starving, into the village's only inn. There, I ate tartiflette for the first time in my life, as if there was no tomorrow. It's not a traditional dish in that particular district (the Reblochon cheese comes from Savoie), but I've never tasted anything as comforting, delicious, and filling as tartiflette together with charcuterie and pickled vegetables. A few minutes later I fell asleep like a baby. Three cheers for the tartiflette, the lifesaver!

9 oz. (250 g) smoked pork loin or bacon, shredded
¼ stick + ⅓ stick (25 g + 30 g) butter
2 banana shallots, finely sliced
1 clove of garlic, finely grated
1 ¾ lb. (800 g) waxy potatoes, peeled and finely sliced
9 oz. (250 g) Reblochon cheese, diced (use Brie if it's difficult to find Reblochon)
1 ½ cups (300 ml) crème fraiche or heavy cream
½ cup (100 ml) dry white wine

Set the oven to 350 °F (180 °C) fan.

Fry the pork loin until crispy in a pan on a medium heat. Remove the pork and leave the fat in the pan.

Add ¼ stick (25 g) of butter to the pan and fry the potatoes, onion, and garlic on low heat without letting it take on color.

Remove and mix the pork, potatoes, cheese, crème fraiche, and wine.

Grease a mold with ⅓ stick (30 g) of butter and pour in the mixture. Bake in the middle of the oven for about 40 minutes, until the tartiflette has a nice color.

Serve with charcuterie and pickled vegetables, or enjoy as it is.

Pan-fried

Some of the top potato dishes appear in this chapter, where we mainly use a frying pan—my best tool. I feel that a frying pan helps to give me a sense of control over my cooking. Browned butter, a hot pan, and potatoes are the foundation for some big things!

One nice thing about cooking potatoes in a frying pan is the speed. You're not cooking things for hours, so you get more bang for your buck. Heat up a pan, add fat, start browning, and off you go.

There's no shame in cooking being a quick affair sometimes. I'm an erratic cook, and the stove is running at full pelt when I'm frying things at home. Every weekend, when I plan to dazzle in the kitchen, the fire alarm goes off and the alarm company calls up to ask what's going on. My family gives the same answer each week, while I stand by the stove oblivious to the red-hot pan on the hot plate. From now on, may I recommend that you all, including myself, remember that there are other stove settings than "maximum." So, turn it down a bit (and also your heart rate). Everything will be tastier, not to mention calmer.

Pan-fried potatoes

There are some memories right here! Mom's pan-fried potatoes would be served with ketchup, mustard, and whatever else. Isn't this the best dish? Of the whole book? So plain and simple, but still top notch.

One of the happiest dishes I know contains fried potatoes: sliced falu sausage fried in butter, fried egg, fried potatoes, mustard, and ketchup. I'm quivering now. I can't think of anything better in the whole world. Maybe there are dishes that are just as good, but definitely not better, and that's an important difference. Always boil too many potatoes!

Cut them up the next day, heat up a pan, add oil, and fry the potatoes until golden brown on a high heat together with some onions. Finish off with butter and eat immediately—leftovers of the very highest order!

1 ¾ lb. (800 g) waxy potatoes, scrubbed
¼ cup (50 ml) canola oil
2 banana shallots or 1 yellow onion, sliced
½ stick (50 g) butter
Salt and freshly ground black pepper

Boil the potatoes in salted water until they're just done. Drain the water, allow the steam to evaporate, and leave to cool completely. You can do this the day before, but it's best when there are leftover potatoes in the fridge.

Cut into the desired shape and size. I go for rough chunks of around 1 inch (2 cm).

Heat up a pan thoroughly. Pour in the oil, add the potatoes, and fry well on one side. Turn and let the potato pieces lie still in the hot fat after each turn so that they have time to get a nice color. Add the onion and butter and fry for a few minutes, until the onion is nice and soft. Season with salt and pepper to taste. Serve immediately.

Raw-fried potatoes

The dish where raw-fried potatoes come into their own is in beef fillet provençale. The beef fillet on top and the garlic butter dripping from the meat into the potatoes would actually be enough of a backdrop for raw-fried potatoes, but it works for other things too.

It's important to slice the potatoes thinly and fry them immediately. Do not rinse them or soak them in water beforehand.

The slices should stick to each other here and there, so that some are lone wolves and others come together in a pack. It's a bit messy to raw-fry as you tend to get the potatoes everywhere. The potatoes will stick to the bottom, even if you have a brand-new pan, and it's difficult to flip them in a dignified way. But keep at it ... it's the fiddling about that's the secret.

Here's the basic recipe and it's possible (no, it's necessary) to experiment with spices and other root vegetables once you've mastered raw-fried potatoes.

1 ¾ lb. (800 g) waxy potatoes, scrubbed
¼ cup (50 ml) canola oil
⅓ stick (30 g) butter
2 cloves of garlic, finely grated
Salt and freshly ground black pepper

Slice the potatoes thinly.

Heat a frying pan to just below maximum temperature. Pour in the oil and butter, add the potatoes and let them fry for a while so that the slices just start to stick to the pan.

Start turning the potatoes and let them fry for a while after each turn. After a few turns, lower the heat slightly, add the garlic, and let the potatoes finish frying and get more color.

Season with salt and pepper and eat immediately.

Crispy potato cakes

There are some potato dishes that are very closely related and easily mixed up: rösti, potato cakes, raggmunk. But there are of course distinct differences. A potato cake is coarsely shredded raw potatoes that are salted and wrung out. Large, thin cakes are then fried directly in the pan, as big as a rösti but much thinner. Raggmunk contains (apart from potatoes) eggs, milk, and flour—there you have the difference in plain sight.

Freshly cooked crispy potato cakes with bleak roe, sour cream or crème fraiche, chopped chives, and red onion. Pair it with an ice-cold beer, and surely there's no one who doesn't like it?

1 ¾ lb. (800 g) waxy potatoes, scrubbed
¼ cup (50 ml) canola oil
½ stick (50 g) butter
Salt

Grate the potatoes on the coarse side of the grater. Season with salt and turn out the potatoes onto a clean kitchen towel that you're not too worried about getting messy.

Heat a pan to just under maximum heat and pour in the oil and butter. Let the butter start to settle and add one quarter of the potatoes in a thin layer. Push out the potato cake while shaking the pan and slide a spatula underneath the potato cake so that it doesn't stick. Bake for about 5 minutes.

Turn and fry until done on the other side. Transfer to a plate, fry three more potato cakes, and serve immediately.

I usually fry potato cakes as big as pancakes, but smaller ones work fine, too.

Hash browns

Hash browns, which have made their way here from the UK and the US, are very similar to our potato cakes, and they get their own mention here because I love them. They're served as a breakfast dish or side dish to various meat and fish dishes. I like that they're so small and cute, almost like the bouncy little siblings of the potato cake. Do the same as for potato cakes but fry them instead as small "plates." A pancake or blini pan is perfect for the job.

Raggmunk

Just like several other potato dishes, the raggmunk potato pancake has its standard accompaniments, namely pork and lingonberries. But it goes with other things, too. Bleak roe for raggmunk is fantastic, but it's with pork and lingonberries that the raggmunk excels. It's doubly good, because when you fry the pork, there's some nice fat left in the pan to fry the raggmunk in, but of course it works with just butter, too. Raggmunks can be made as small as dishes or as large as the entire frying pan. I haven't actually decided what I like best... it varies each time. I also add a little sugar to the batter to get a nicer color and a better crunch.

You need sweetened lingonberries for the raggmunk and pork. At one unfortunate dinner at home, I had roasted the pork, made the raggmunks, and was strutting merrily towards the refrigerator to get the sweetened lingonberries that I knew with absolute certainty were there. Except they weren't. It had all been used on that morning's porridge. The feeling of grief was incomparable. I can't remember which jam we used instead. My brain went haywire due to the disconnect between flavor and consistency, and it almost became the last time I ate raggmunk with pork.

3 eggs
1 cup (120 g) wheat flour
1 ¼ cup (250 ml) whole milk
1 tsp. salt
½ tbsp. granulated sugar
1 lb. (400 g) waxy potatoes, peeled
1 stick (100 g) butter for frying and any pork fat
Sweetened lingonberries—see the recipe on page 103

Mix the eggs and wheat flour into a thick mass. Whisk in the milk, salt, and sugar.

Roughly grate the potato and let it drain in a colander. It doesn't need to be wrung out. Fold the potatoes into the batter.

Heat a frying pan to just below maximum heat. Add the butter and any pork fat. Pour out batter for the size you want. Fry the raggmunks until golden brown and crispy at the edges. Turn and fry the other side until done as well. Serve immediately with pork and lingonberries.

Rösti

Switzerland is the birthplace of the rösti, where it's eaten for breakfast, lunch, and dinner, and is made with love in many forms, primarily in German-speaking areas. There are countless variations of rösti—with smoked pork, cheese, or lots of onions. I make mine with smoked pork loin, lots of onions, and a little garlic. There needs to be a kick in my rösti!

A long time ago I worked with someone from Switzerland. The pride when we would make a rösti was unimaginable. There was an extra pride in being able to flip it in the air (I've never understood why) and there was considerable drama the first time I made a rösti. I made a large rösti in the widest frying pan and managed to turn the 11 lbs. (5 kg) thing reasonably well! But when it came time for my companion from the Alps to show us how it should be done, the damned thing landed on the edge at the exact moment that our extremely strict chef entered the kitchen.

Fortunately, both spoke German and were able to work things out in their own language. I remember, during those seconds of heated debate in German, suddenly becoming very interested in something on my cutting board. A couple of weeks after the incident, we were still finding potato shavings in every thinkable (and unthinkable) place in the kitchen. Ever since, everyone knows whether I turn my rösti in the air or whether I use a plate. Yeah, you guessed right.

Rösti can be made with boiled or raw potatoes, both are considered correct. I go with boiled, because I think it's tastier and creamier. In addition, the difference between the rösti and the potato cake becomes more distinct, although the potato cake is admittedly thinner.

1 ¾ lb. (800 g) waxy potatoes, scrubbed
3 yellow onions
½ clove of garlic, finely grated
½ stick + ¼ stick (50 g + 25 g) butter
3 tbsp. canola oil
4 oz. (100 g) smoked pork loin, finely shredded (bacon also works well)
Salt and freshly ground black pepper

Boil the potatoes in salted water until they're just done. Drain the water, allow the steam to evaporate, and leave to cool.

Cook the onion and garlic until soft in ¼ stick (25 g) of butter.

Grate the potatoes on the coarse side of the grater. Heat a frying pan to slightly below max. Pour in oil and add ½ stick (50 g) of butter, and let the butter melt until it stops sizzling in the oil. Add the potatoes, onions, and pork loin. Season with salt and pepper. Turn around for a few minutes while the potatoes fry in the fat and then press down to form a nice cake.

Shake the pan constantly and loosen it a little at the edges with a spatula so that the rösti doesn't stick. Fry for 5 to 10 minutes on a medium heat.

Once the underside has a nice color, turn the cake by placing a large plate on the pan and quickly turning it upside down so that the rösti ends up on the plate. Put the rösti back in the pan with the golden-brown side up and fry until the other side is nicely browned as well.

Put the rösti on a nice plate or serve directly from the pan.

Top to bottom: Potato cake, Raggmunk, Rösti.

Potato buns

A bit of potato cake, a bit of raggmunk, a bit of lufsa, and a bit of rösti. And there you have your background to the potato bun. Leftovers are great for cooking, and a lunch or dinner of potato buns made from yesterday's leftovers is always a hit. It works great on its own as a vegetarian dish, or with accompaniments such as pork, bacon, or a piece of fish. But it's also worth boiling some potatoes just to make this delicacy. Just make sure the potatoes are completely cool before you grate them. Otherwise, it can easily become sticky, and the batter can be too loose if the potatoes are freshly cooked and still lukewarm.

2 ¼ lb. (1 kg) waxy potatoes, boiled
½ stick (50 g) butter, browned
2 yellow onions, finely chopped
2 eggs
Salt
½ cup (50 g) breadcrumbs
3 tbsp. canola oil

If you have cold boiled potatoes, grate them on the coarse side of the grater directly into a bowl. If you freshly boil potatoes, let them cool completely in the refrigerator before grating them.

Sauté the onion in the butter until soft and mix with the potatoes. Add the eggs and salt. Mix everything together and use lightly floured hands to form balls of the dough. Press the balls and coat them in breadcrumbs.

Heat a pan to just below maximum heat. Add oil and a little butter. Let the butter settle down and then fry the potato buns until golden brown on both sides.

Farmer's omelet

A tasty omelet served open. Unlike a traditional omelet, which is folded in the pan, this is left open, round, and beautiful. Actually, I don't have any exact ingredients when I make my farmer's omelet. I just throw in what I have at home in the refrigerator. I don't understand why it's called a farmer's omelet, but I guess it's because it's a bit rough around the edges. It's everything you need after a hard day's work, and few people work as hard as farmers.

For me, it's important that the omelet is creamy and a little runny in the middle. It just makes it that little extra bit special.

1 large omelet

1 lb. (400 g) waxy potatoes, scrubbed
5 tbsp. canola oil
8 oz. (200 g) smoked pork loin or bacon, in rough pieces
2 yellow onions, sliced
1 leek, finely sliced
1 clove of garlic, finely sliced
8 eggs
Salt and freshly ground black pepper
1 bunch parsley, coarsely chopped

Boil the potatoes just until ready in salted water and allow to cool slightly.

Cut into rough pieces, about 1 inch (2 cm) in size.

Heat a large pan to just below maximum heat. Pour in the oil and fry the pork until crispy.

Lower the heat and add the potatoes, onions, leeks, and garlic. Sauté on a low heat for about 5 minutes without it taking color.

Crack the eggs into a bowl and quickly whisk together into a batter, season with salt and pepper. Pour the batter into the pan and stir for a couple of minutes. Then let the mixture "sit" on a low heat without stirring for about 5 minutes.

Sprinkle with the parsley and serve immediately.

Potato tortilla

For those of you who've just joined us, we're talking about potatoes. We're reached the potato tortilla, or Spanish tortilla as it's also called. Just like Switzerland's rösti, tortillas are eaten in Spain for breakfast, lunch, and dinner, and they're just as good hot or cold. The tortilla has burst into my life with a bang. I always make a big one that stays in the fridge and I cut some from it during the day. I like to serve freshly made tortilla with thin slices of charcuterie.

It's important to slice the potatoes thinly and not rinse them or leave them in water before cooking. The potatoes stick a little when you fry them, so just like with raw-fried potatoes, you can simply keep turning the potatoes even though they'll stick. I use a well-seasoned cast iron pan and first pan-fry the potatoes in a lot of oil until they become soft. Then I put the potatoes in a bowl and fry the onion and garlic in the pan with the same oil, without letting them take any color. I crack the eggs and mix them into a batter that I leave to rest before I fry the tortilla until golden brown on both sides. This is culinary craftsmanship at its finest.

1 ¾ lb. (800 g) waxy potatoes, peeled and finely sliced
¼ cup + ¼ cup (50 ml + 50 ml) olive oil
¼ cup (50 ml) canola oil
2 banana shallots, finely sliced
2 cloves of garlic, finely grated
4 eggs + possibly 2 extra egg yolks
Salt and freshly ground black pepper

Heat a frying pan to medium heat and pour in ¼ cup (50 ml) of olive oil, canola oil, and potatoes. Season with salt and pepper. Pan-fry the potatoes until soft on a medium heat for about 10 minutes without letting them take any color. Turn the potatoes a few times in the meantime.

Pour the potatoes into a bowl using a slotted spoon, being careful to bring as little oil over as possible. Fry the onion and garlic until soft in the same pan, remove, and mix with the potatoes.

Clean the pan.

Crack the eggs (and 2 extra egg yolks for maximum creaminess) into the potatoes, coat well, and let the batter rest for about 15 minutes. Season the batter with salt and pepper just before frying.

Heat the pan again, add ¼ cup (50 ml) of olive oil, and pour in the potato batter. Fry the tortilla on a medium heat until it's golden brown on one side, which will take around 5 to 8 minutes. Turn the tortilla using a plate and fry until golden brown and done on the other side as well.

Serve the tortilla on a plate. Serve immediately or let it cool and serve later on.

Tortilla Vaga, thin potato tortilla

A thin tortilla similar to a regular potato tortilla. I just have to include this variant as well. It's a veritable dream that's too damn good to be left out of this book. Just like a normal potato tortilla, the thin tortilla has sliced potatoes, but here the tortilla is fried thin on a high heat like an open omelet and puffs up at the edges from the heat. It should be properly creamy in the middle and not completely solid. You can top your thin tortilla with your choice of goodies such as spicy sausage, charcuterie, or vegetables. I also have my own Swedified version, which I top with shredded cold-smoked salmon, sautéed onions, pickled mustard seeds, and dill. Or bleak roe. Or ... well, you get the idea. You can make this tortilla whichever way you want. Then place it on the table and cut slices that people can take as they please, or cook a large one and it eat yourself for lunch.

I do one more thing that's different, but quite common in Spain—I replace the sliced fried potatoes with chips. So you just beat together eggs, add a little salt, and either turn in homemade chips or store-bought salted chips, and then fry your thin tortilla. It may sound strange, but it gives a very special texture and is a handy trick! You can even use chips in a regular tortilla, too, but they work best in the thin kind.

4 appetizer servings

2 oz. (60 g) potato chips, homemade or bought
4 eggs
Pinch of salt
¼ cup (50 ml) olive oil

Whisk the eggs and salt together in a bowl. Pour in the chips.

Heat a pan thoroughly, pour in the olive oil, and let it get smoking hot.

Pour the batter into the pan and make sure it puffs up nicely at the edges. Work with the heat by lifting the pan from time to time and feel if the tortilla has started to solidify. It should stay nicely creamy and be almost runny in the middle.

Turn the tortilla upside down on a plate so that the creamy side faces up. Top with whatever you want, such as charcuterie and pickled vegetables, cold-smoked salmon and/or bleak roe with onions, pickled mustard seeds, and dill.

Tuttul, potato flatbread

This bread has a special place in my life and I've had it on the menu ever since I started my restaurant. In our version, we prove the bread during the evening and bake it when we get an order. The bread is served warm, with our own butter and jam.

Freshly baked bread, which is so hot that you almost burn yourself on it, is close to many people's hearts. A bit cliché, but true. All around Sweden, different types of flat bread are baked, but it's only the tuttul bread from Rättvik that uses potatoes. The bread takes on a special character, juicy and rich. I'll never get tired of my tuttul.

Try making salmon tartare. Put it on the bread, fold them up like small tacos, and serve as a snack. Wonderful!

24 portions of bread

Step 1

½ oz. (15 g) yeast
2 tbsp. granulated sugar
½ stick (50 g) butter
1 ¼ cup (250 ml) whole milk
3 tbsp. honey
1 tsp. whole aniseed
1 tsp. fennel seeds
2 tsp. salt
1 ½ cups (180 g) sifted rye flour
1 ½ cups (180 g) wheat flour

Step 2

¾ lb. (300 g) waxy potatoes, ideally Annika, boiled and pressed
¾ cup (90 g) sifted rye flour
2 ½ cups (300 g) wheat flour

Step 1: Crumble the yeast in a bowl and add the sugar. Melt the butter and pour in the milk, honey, spices, and salt. Heat to 100 °F (37 °C). Pour the liquid over the yeast and stir well. Add the rye flour and wheat flour. Stir together to form a sticky dough and leave covered with a tea towel at room temperature for around 1 ½ hours.

Step 2: Add the potatoes, rye flour, and wheat flour. Work them together quickly with a dough hook or by hand on a table to form the dough. Roll the dough into a fine roll. Divide the dough into 24 pieces and roll out each piece with a little extra flour into a "loaf" about 8 inches (20 cm) in diameter. Place greaseproof paper between each round and freeze or leave to rise for an hour before frying. If you're going to pan-fry frozen bread, take it out of the freezer 2 hours before and let it come to room temperature.

Heat a frying pan to maximum heat. Fry the bread quickly in a dry pan for about 1 minute on each side. Serve the bread immediately, as it's best when freshly baked.

Potato crêpes

Crêpes vonnassiennes is the most famous dish served by the great French three-star chef Georges Blanc at his tavern in Vonnas. He serves his potato crêpes with caviar and salmon. They're a bit reminiscent of blini and I'm guessing they were the inspiration when the crêpes were invented. These are not crêpes in the way you normally think of crêpes, which are more like potato pancakes. I'm skeptical of blini and like these better if I can bring myself to eat caviar or if I want something different with bleak roe.

¾ lb. (300 g) waxy potatoes, peeled
2 eggs
1 cup (200 ml) crème fraiche
1 cup (120 g) wheat flour
3 egg whites
Butter for frying

Boil the potatoes in salted water and press them straight into a bowl.

Mix in the eggs, crème fraiche, and wheat flour. It should be a thick batter, but keep in mind that the amount of starch in potatoes varies, so you may need a little more crème fraiche or flour than the recipe calls for.

Beat the egg whites into a stiff foam and fold into the potato batter. Griddle some nice rounds in butter in a frying pan.

These are great served with bleak roe, sour cream, and chopped red onion, but also with caviar.

Potato pancakes

No, this isn't a raggmunk, nor is it a potato bun. It's the same story with the potato waffle on page 152. Sometimes you just want to eat pancakes or waffles for dinner or lunch, and then you can sneak some goodies into the batter so that the children (and the adults) at least get some nutrition. Also, it's not raw potatoes like in raggmunk, but boiled. Another tip is to try shredding potatoes into an oven pancake.

Perfect leftovers, so always save boiled potatoes. Lingonberries and lightly whipped cream are the best partners for the potato pancake, but they can also be used to make hearty crêpes. Set them to one side when they've cooled, roll them up, lay tightly in an oven dish, and gratinate.

Approx. 10 pancakes

1 lb. (400 g) waxy potatoes, peeled
3 eggs
1 ½ cups (180 g) wheat flour
3 cups (600 ml) whole milk
½ tsp. salt
Butter for frying

Boil the potatoes in salted water and leave to cool. Coarsely grate the potatoes.

Whisk the eggs and flour together in a bowl into a thick batter. Add the milk, a little at a time, and beat until smooth. Season with salt and fold the potatoes into the batter.

Griddle the pancakes in a pan with plenty of butter.

Potato waffles

You're not having waffles for dinner, are you!? Do you recognize that question? I imagine it's because waffles or pancakes can be a bit lightweight when it comes to their nutritional value, and maybe a little bit too decadent. But life is to be lived, so I turn the other way sometimes. And if you want to squeeze in something a little nutritious, there's always the potato waffle. Lighter than regular waffles and, of course, tastier and more compatible with fancier toppings than just jam and cream. Perfect for kids and kids at heart. The kids can top them with jam and cream, while the adults can slap on a tasty topping like Skagen, Öjeby, or Sikafors mix, or simply some bleak roe.

About 10 waffles

¾ lb. (300 g) floury potatoes, peeled
1 cup (200 ml) whole milk
2 cups (240 g) wheat flour
1 cup (200 ml) carbonated water
2 eggs
1 tsp. baking powder
1 tsp. salt
1 ½ stick (150 g) butter +
Melted butter for griddling

Boil the potatoes in salted water until they're just done. Drain the water and allow to cool completely.

Melt 1 ½ stick (150 g) butter. Whisk together the milk, carbonated water, wheat flour, eggs, baking powder, and salt. Add the butter.

Heat the waffle maker. Coarsely grate the potato and mix it into the batter. Griddle some nice waffles, using around ½ cup (100 ml) of batter for each waffle.

Skagen mix

2 egg yolks
1 tbsp. Dijon mustard
2 tsp. white wine vinegar
1 ½ cups (300 ml) canola oil
Juice of ½ lemon
1 lb. (400 g) peeled fresh prawns, roughly split
Bleak roe or other roe of your choice
½ bunch dill
Salt

Whisk together the egg yolks, mustard, and vinegar in a bowl. Add the oil in a thin stream while whisking the mayonnaise until creamy and fine. Season with salt and lemon juice to taste.

Coat the prawns in the mayonnaise. Spoon the mixture over freshly baked waffle hearts and top with bleak roe and picked dill.

Öjeby mix

18 oz. (500 g) peeled crayfish tails in brine, carefully declawed and coarsely chopped
4 oz. (100 g) Västerbotten cheese or any other mature cheese, grated
1 tbsp. whole cumin, pounded in a mortar
½ cup (100 ml) mayonnaise, bought or see the recipe for Skagen above
Finely grated zest of 1 lemon
1 fl. oz. (30 ml) aquavit
2 tbsp. finely chopped dill

Mix all the ingredients in a bowl and leave in the fridge for a few hours.

Top the freshly baked waffle hearts with the mixture.

Sikafors mix—see the recipe on page 92.

Deep-fried

Two things are imperative here.

1: That you deep-fry safely when using oil.

2: That the oil is nice and clean so you don't make your home smell like a decrepit old diner.

Anyone who starts deep-frying and intends to do so a little more often would do best to get a deep fryer. It's so much better and safer, not to mention the smell. I'm a fan of the deep fryer. When coupled with good oil and the right method, the result is anything but the heavy food dripping-in-grease that many people associate with deep-fried food.

Instead, you get incredible crispiness and crunch and some magical things happen with the potatoes. The deep fryer can become a real friend in the kitchen that can be used for many things. You can deep-fry in a pan as well, of course, but you have to be more careful with the oil and it won't have quite the same effect.

Make sure you always have good oil at home, as it really does make all the difference. Don't use the same oil too many times, strain it between each use and buy organic.

There are some real gems in this chapter, such as french fries and chips. Then there's patatas bravas, one of the tastiest things in the potato kingdom.

French fries

French fries must be the most-eaten potato dish in the world by far. It also has to be the potato dish that everyone likes, that works with everything, and that everyone has a clear reference to. So, it must also be the potato dish that's the most difficult to impress others with when you prepare it yourself.

The fries served in restaurants, street kitchens, and burger chains are usually so good that they're hard to beat. But if you manage to make good fries at home? Hats off to you! Well done!

The biggest challenge is to get the crunch. I'm nervous every time I make fries at home. The crunch ... it's the crunch that is the measure of my success. But how do you achieve it? There are countless methods. I've figured out the best one by sneaking into various street kitchens and checking out the bags of ready-made fries, and the answer is clear (because it's usually written on the bags): Pre-boil, pre-fry, and freeze. It's no more difficult than that. Shred floury potatoes straight into cold water for rinsing, then pre-boil for about three minutes, fry once, and freeze quickly. The freezing itself causes water crystals to form, which helps to improve the texture of the potatoes when they're fried. In addition, the surface dries during freezing, which is very important for the crunch.

When it's time to serve, I take the fries out of the freezer and fry them at a high temperature until they're crunchy as hell. Salt and serve, period.

It may seem complicated and ambitious, but it's just a matter of getting stuck in. Make a big batch, store them in the freezer, and take them out and deep-fry them when you feel like it.

The absolute best thing to do with fries is dip them in really good homemade mayonnaise. I'll gladly give readers my mayo recipe. Make it at the same time as you make your crunchy fries and let the ecstasy wash over you.

1 ¾ lb. (800 g) floury potatoes, ideally at least 4 inches (10 cm) in diameter, scrubbed
8 cups (2 l) water
3 tbsp. vinegar
1 tbsp. salt
Frying oil

Bring the water, vinegar, and salt to a boil.

Shred the potatoes and rinse under cold running water.

Pre-boil the strips for 2 to 3 minutes in the vinegar water and cool in ice water.

Heat the frying oil to 285 °F (140 °C). Dry the potato strips well on a kitchen towel and fry in batches for around 5 minutes until nicely colored.

Remove the strips and cool slightly before spreading out on a plate or tray lined with greaseproof paper and freeze them quickly.

Once frozen, store them in plastic bags in the freezer until needed. Fry for a second time before serving.

When serving: Remove from the the freezer and fry until crispy and golden brown in hot oil at 360 °F (180 °C).

Remove, drain quickly on kitchen paper, season with salt, and serve.

Mayonnaise

2 egg yolks
2 tbsp. Dijon mustard
1 tbsp. white wine vinegar
1 ½ cups (300 ml) neutral canola oil
Juice of 1 lemon
Salt

Whisk together the egg yolks, mustard, and vinegar in a bowl. Add the oil in a thin stream while constantly whisking. Season to taste with salt and lemon juice if you want extra acidity.

Shoestring potatoes

Shoestring potatoes, or matchstick potatoes as they're also known, are the mischievous little sibling of French fries, but messy and disheveled like they've just woken up. Unlike French fries, shoestring potatoes are more akin to chips, although shoestring potatoes work as an accompaniment to more dishes than chips. They're also great as a snack and you can just let people dig in with their hands.

Shoestring potatoes can be fried in advance and served later. They last several days in an airtight jar stored at room temperature, although they're best freshly fried.

½ cup (75 g) salt
1 ¾ lb. (800 g) floury potatoes, peeled
8 ½ cups (2 l) water
Frying oil

Warm the water to around 150 °F (65 °C). Whisk in the salt and keep the water lukewarm.

Slice the potatoes thinly on a mandoline (about ⅛ inch/3 mm) and then into fine strips with a knife. Place the strips directly in the water and leave to soak for 15 minutes.

Let the strips drain in a colander. Then place the strips on a clean kitchen towel and pat dry. Fry the strips in batches in oil heated to 330 °F (165 °C) until they're crispy and golden brown. Gently stir using steel kitchen tongs. Remove the strips and place on paper towels to drain well.

Add extra salt on top and serve immediately, or leave to cool and store in a box with a tight-fitting lid at room temperature.

Chips

It may sound trite, but my love for potatoes in general is rooted in my unreserved love for chips. Sure, I could go on and on about how, as a child, I had an epiphany from some potato dish that I've loved ever since. But the truth is, it's chips. Nowadays I love anything with potatoes, but in the beginning it was chips.

Chips are sold in their droves worldwide. I know they're not nutritious and it takes huge quantities of potatoes and an enormous amount of energy to produce them, but I love them all the same. My dream is to make my own and sell them, with my own unique flavors. One day, maybe.

When I make chips, I use the same technique as for fries in that I don't heat the potato slices for as long but I use the same brine. Feel free to experiment with different potato varieties. Almond potatoes are great for chips, maybe even the best. They're starchy, floury, and just wonderful.

In terms of seasoning, there are really only two worth mentioning: dill and black pepper. For dill chips, I sprinkle dried dill on the chips just as soon as they are out of the fryer.

It's the same for black pepper, just use a pepper mill to grind it onto the freshly fried chips.

And then you have the dips. I actually think that homemade chips, both flavored and plain, are really nice to eat as they are, without dip. That said, on certain occasions, for natural chips I make my best dip: Västerbotten dip.

Previous pages: Chips, three favorites—lightly salted, dill, and black pepper.

1 ¾ lb. (800 g) floury potatoes, scrubbed
8 ½ cups (2 l) water
2 cups (400 ml) white wine vinegar
½ cup (75 g) salt
Frying oil

Heat the water, vinegar, and salt to boiling point.

Slice the potatoes thinly using a mandoline and put in ice water for 20 minutes.

Place the potatoes in the hot vinegar water using a slotted spoon. Turn down the heat and let the potatoes soak in the water at about 200 °F (90 °C) for about 15 minutes.

Remove the slices with a slotted spoon and place in ice water again for about 15 minutes.

Strain off the water and dry the slices well using a kitchen towel.

Fry the slices in batches in oil heated to 330 °F (165 °C) until they're crispy and golden brown. Remove the slices using a slotted spoon and place on paper towels to drain. Salt and season with dried dill or black pepper if you wish.

Serve immediately, or store in a box with a tight-fitting lid at room temperature.

Dried dill
1 bunch dill, picked

Set the oven to 150 °F (65 °C) no fan.

Place the dill on a baking tray lined with baking paper. Put the tray in the oven and leave for about 3 hours.

Remove the tray from the oven. Mix and sieve the dill and sprinkle it over the chips.

Västerbotten dip
1 cup (200 ml) sour cream
½ cup (100 g) finely grated Västerbotten cheese or any other mature cheese
Finely grated zest of ½ lemon
1 tsp. ground cumin
Salt

Whisk the dip ingredients together in a bowl and season with salt.

When you want a dip, make Västerbotten dip. Then you'll have something with a real kick.

Fried potato skins

I'm not looking to overcomplicate things here. It's good to take advantage of everything that nature provides and it's a good use of resources to use up leftovers. In fact, I make chips out of potato skins because they're tasty, fun, and easy when you know how. You can make these crispy skins mid-week and store them in an airtight container until the weekend to have as an ace up your sleeve when serving some impressive snacks.

I peel or tourne (see page 25) the potatoes and put the skins straight into cold water, leaving them there in the same way as when I make regular chips (see page 162). There's nothing stopping anyone from making lovely crispy potato skins that can be saved for a Friday treat!

I love to serve the shells with the best dip on earth ... feta mayonnaise. Feta cheese is the new Parmesan!

1 ¾ lb. (800 g) potato skins from waxy or floury potatoes
8 cups (2 l) water
2 cups (400 ml) white wine vinegar
½ cup (75 g) salt
Frying oil

Heat the water, vinegar, and salt to boiling point.

Place the potato skins in ice water for 20 minutes, and then in the hot vinegar water using a slotted spoon. Turn down the heat and let the skins soak in the water at about 200 °F (90 °C) for about 15 minutes.

Remove the skins with a slotted spoon and place in ice water again for about 15 minutes.

Strain off the water and dry the skins well using a kitchen towel. Fry the skins in 330 °F (165 °C) oil until golden brown and crispy.

Serve immediately, or store in a box with a tight-fitting lid at room temperature.

Feta mayo

2 ½ oz. (75 g) feta cheese
1 ¼ cup (250 ml) canola oil
2 egg yolks
2 tbsp. Dijon mustard
1 tbsp. white wine vinegar
1 clove of garlic, finely grated
Zest of 1 lemon and squeezed juice
Salt

Mix the rapeseed oil and feta cheese until smooth.

Whisk together the egg yolks, mustard, vinegar, lemon zest, and garlic in a bowl. Add the feta oil in a thin stream while whisking. Season to taste with salt and lemon juice if you want extra acidity.

Patatas bravas

In Sweden, it's peanuts that are our snack of choice with a beer at the bar, but in Spain it's patatas bravas. This dish is quite versatile and can be enjoyed as both a bar snack and a tapas dish. It conjures images of the sun, Spain, warm days, cold drinks, and a bowl of crispy potatoes with a potent sauce. Eaten with your hands, it becomes wonderfully sticky food to get messy with.

"Bravas" roughly translates as "strong" or "brave," and hints at the sauce that adorns the potatoes. I step things up a bit for even better texture and more kick, and make a smooth aioli that I drizzle over the potatoes as generously as the bravas sauce.

As everyone knows, kebab meat is best enjoyed with both red and white sauce, and the same applies to patatas bravas.

1 ¾ lb. (800 g) floury potatoes, scrubbed and halved
Oil for frying
Salt

Boil the potato wedges for about 5 minutes in salted water. Remove and cool in ice water.

Dry the potatoes well and pre-fry in hot oil at 285 °F (140 °C) for about 10 minutes. Remove using a slotted spoon and place on paper towels to drain and cool.

Fry the potatoes a second time in hot oil at 340 °F (170 °C) until crispy and golden brown. Remove using a slotted spoon and place on paper towels to drain. Pile the potatoes on plates. Drizzle generously with both sauces and serve immediately with extra sauce on the side.

See the recipe for potato aioli on page 78.

Bravas sauce

2 tbsp. hot paprika powder
1 tbsp. smoked paprika powder
⅓ cup (80 ml) olive oil
1 tbsp. wheat flour
1 ¼ cup (250 ml) chicken broth
Salt

Sauté the paprika powder in the olive oil at a medium-high temperature for a few minutes. Add the flour and sauté for another minute. Pour in the broth a little at a time while constantly whisking. Once all the broth has been added, the sauce should boil for about 10 minutes to a consistency that's good for drizzling over the potatoes. Strain the sauce, season with salt, and serve lukewarm or cold.

Fried Hasselback potatoes

You could almost say that this potato changed my life. There's a time before and a time after I started making this snack.

I thought for a long time about doing something with Hasselback potatoes—a dish I adore even when cooked traditionally. My idea was a finger-friendly snack that would feel authentic, but also be ultra-modern, light, and damn yummy. It took forever to find the ultimate recipe. We worked on it for six months and almost gave up. I freaked out and put it on hold a few times before finally landing upon this.

The dish has become a symbol of the Hantverket restaurant and I'm incredibly grateful for that. It has also changed my life, both practically and physically. I've probably made 6 or 7 million incisions since we started on the project. I can get almost the same feeling when cutting Hasselback potatoes as I do when I get tired behind the wheel of a car and have to stop. Your eyelids become incredibly heavy and you just want to collapse.

But there's no danger to life here ... I can cut and sleep at the same time. No, really. Sometimes I just stand and cut the potatoes with my eyes closed.

4 servings as snacks

12 small waxy potatoes, scrubbed
4 tbsp. sour cream
2 oz. (60 g) bleak roe
½ bunch dill, picked and roughly chopped
1 scallion, finely sliced
Frying oil

Brine
4 cups (1 l) water
1 cup (200 ml) apple cider vinegar
½ cup (75 g) salt

Slice the potatoes finely, almost all the way through. Use either a wooden spoon or a towel that's folded three times from each side to form a "trough" in the middle to place the potatoes into.

Put the potatoes immediately in ice water once you've cut them.

Boil the water, vinegar, and salt in a pot. Put the potatoes in and simmer in the water at around 200 °F (90 °C) for 1 hour without a lid and without letting the water bubble. The potatoes should be a little soft but not cooked through, almost half-raw. The potatoes mustn't boil and mustn't be fully cooked. Remove the potatoes with a slotted spoon and leave to cool in ice water. The potatoes can be prepared up to this point up to 3 days before serving.

When serving: Remove the potatoes from the water and let them drain slightly. Fry in absolutely clean oil for 25 to 30 minutes at 285 °F (140 °C) until the potatoes are crispy all the way through. But keep an eye on it—it may take more time or less. The potatoes will almost start to bubble when they're ready.

Remove the potatoes and place on a wire rack or on paper towels to drain.

If you have time, you can continue cooking the fried potatoes in an oven at 150 °F (65 °C) for an hour to make them even crispier. The potatoes can be left in the oven for a maximum of 2 hours. If you're short on time, you can skip this step.

Top with the sour cream, bleak roe, dill, and scallions. Serve immediately.

This beloved Hasselback potato has changed my life.

Pommes dauphine

This classic French potato side dish is a must if you want to delve into the innermost workings of potato-based cuisine. When I started working as a chef, pommes dauphine were produced with precision in every kitchen and knowledge of the method was mandatory. Equally important were pommes lorette, which are made from the same dough but shaped differently.

The basis is a choux batter, or a fire dough as it was once called, which is mixed with boiled pressed potatoes. Dauphine is shaped into small balls or eggs, while lorette is piped into a wreath. When the dough is made this way, it holds together without breading during frying and the surface becomes crispy. It's a real showstopper for the Sunday roast or for grilling in the summer.

⅓ stick (30 g) butter
4 ½ oz. (125 g) wheat flour
2 eggs
1 lb. (400 g) floury potatoes, peeled
1 cup (250 ml) water
Freshly grounded nutmeg
Oil for frying
Salt and freshly ground black pepper

Boil the water and butter in a pot. Fold in the flour with a wooden spoon and stir constantly while keeping the pan on the stove. The dough should become hot and eventually pull away from the sides of the pan. Once the dough has loosened, let it brown lightly for a few minutes, stirring constantly.

Move the pan aside and add the eggs, one at a time while continuing to stir vigorously with the wooden spoon.

Boil the potatoes in salted water and press them straight away. Mix the potatoes with the choux batter and season with salt, pepper, and nutmeg. Make balls or eggs from the dough. To form nice eggs, take two tablespoons, preferably slightly pointed, and shape the batter between them by passing it back and forth. It helps if you dip the spoons in hot oil between making each egg. Place the eggs on parchment paper and let cool. To make lorette, pipe wreaths onto parchment paper using a cloth piping bag and let cool.

Fry a few eggs at a time in 330 °F (170 °C) hot frying oil until golden brown. Drain quickly on kitchen paper and serve.

Potato croutons

I came up with this dish in a hurry when I was making raggmunk at home one day. All of a sudden, the recipe fell into my lap as I was shredding potatoes. I grate the potatoes very finely, salt them, and wring out the liquid in a towel. It's incredibly important to get most of the liquid out for a good end result. Then I mix the grated potato with beaten egg and bake everything in a plastic mold and leave to cool completely. The recipe can be prepared well in advance and it's really convenient.

When serving, I cut the baked potatoes into cubes, as big as I feel like at the time, and deep-fry them until crispy. The croutons are like little mini raggmunks and are insanely tasty in starters with herring and bleak roe. Almost anything with fish, actually. They can also be cut into larger pieces, deep-fried, and served with a main course with meat. The plain version is your starting point, from which you can add whatever flavors you can think of—cheese, spices, shredded vegetables—and mix them with the potatoes. There are no problems here, you see ... only solutions.

1 ¾ lb. (800 g) waxy potatoes, peeled
2 eggs
½ cup (100 ml) heavy cream
Grated zest of 1 lemon
Salt
Oil for frying

Set the oven to 250 °F (120 °C) fan. Grate the potatoes finely and salt them.

Place the gratings in a clean kitchen towel that you're not worried about getting messy and wring out as much liquid as possible.

Mix the eggs, cream, lemon zest, and salt. Pour the mixture into the wrung-out potatoes and put everything in a plastic baking mold 8 × 8 inches in size (about 20 × 20 cm). Fold over the plastic that is hanging over the edges. If necessary, put some plastic film on top of everything without it ending up on the edge of the mold. Fold the plastic wrap toward the center if it's too large.

Bake in the middle of the oven for about 45 minutes or until the internal temperature of the patty is 208 °F (98 °C). Remove and leave to cool completely at room temperature and then store in the refrigerator.

When serving, remove and cut into cubes. Deep-fry a few at a time in 350 °F (175 °C) oil until nicely golden brown. Remove using a slotted spoon, place on paper towels to drain, and serve.

Potato croquettes

Perfect potatoes for an easy dinner at home. Can be prepared in advance and then take out of the freezer to deep-fry before serving when you need to boost your mood. A tasty accompaniment to a variety of dishes, or as a snack with a good mayo (see pages 156 or 164) or potato aioli (see page 78). I can't think of anyone who doesn't like a potato croquette!

First comes the crunch, followed by hot mashed potato that absorbs any sauce or dip like nothing else. Once you've mastered the recipe, you can let your imagination run wild when it comes to flavors. I like to chop some cold-smoked salmon into the batter, a lot of fried mushrooms, or maybe a half-potato half-artichoke mix? Don't hold back!

1 ¾ lb. (800 g) waxy potatoes, scrubbed
1 ½ oz. (40 g) mature cheese, grated
3 shallots, finely chopped
2 cloves of garlic, finely grated
Grated zest of 1 lemon
½ bunch flat leaf parsley, roughly chopped
½ stick (50 g) butter
Cornstarch
2 eggs
Panko
Salt and freshly ground black pepper

Boil the potatoes in salted water until they're just done and immediately mash them with a fork.

Soften the onion, garlic, and lemon peel in the butter for about 5 minutes and mix into the potatoes. Add the parsley and cheese and season with salt and pepper, then leave to cool slightly.

Roll into balls, about an inch (2–3 cm) in diameter. Bread the balls first in cornstarch, then in beaten egg, and finally in panko.

Deep-fry a few balls at a time in 350 °F (175 °C) oil until golden brown. Place on paper towels to drain and serve, preferably with the potato aioli on page 78.

Pommes Williams

The crunchiest potato in the book? The basis is mashed potatoes, much like duchess potatoes, which are mixed with onions, bacon, and parsley and then shaped like pears before being breaded and deep-fried. I've researched the origin of this dish and believe me, it's not easy! I can't speak for pommes Williams, but no one can help but be happy with some perfectly fried potato pears.

1¾ lb. (800 g) waxy potatoes, scrubbed
3 oz. (80 g) bacon, finely diced
½ stick (50 g) butter
3 shallots, finely chopped
2 cloves of garlic, finely grated
½ bunch flat leaf parsley, roughly chopped
Cornstarch
2 eggs
Panko
Oil for frying
Salt and freshly ground black pepper
8 cloves, as "stems" for the pear croquettes

Boil the potatoes in salted water until they're just done and immediately mash them with a fork.

Fry the bacon until crispy but not burnt and drain on paper towels. Cook the onion and garlic in the butter until soft, for around 5 minutes.

Mix the bacon and onion into the mashed potatoes, add the parsley, and season with salt and pepper. Allow to cool slightly.

Shape the potato batter into pears, two per person. Bread the pears first in cornstarch, then in beaten egg, and finally in panko. Deep-fry until golden brown in 350 °F (175 °C) oil. Drain a little on kitchen paper and serve.

TUME
VOLVO
Krabat

Potato passionistas

The wise old chap and the potato field

I have a picture in my head of me walking alongside fields. I look out over the fields and see my potato plants standing verdant and proud, waiting to be earthed-up. Suddenly, I turn off the dirt road into one of the fields, step in, pull up a plant, and study my potatoes. I am one with the potato. The wise old chap in his potato field. I drive a tractor, plant potatoes in the spring, worry about the weather, and fertilize, water, and harvest my crops. My life in the field.

But it's not like that. I'm not a seasoned potato farmer. No, the kitchen is enough for me, and that's where we find this wise old chap. But it's a nice goal to have! I want to grow, learn more, and be close to those who live off the land, those who can. I want to know everything. What's life like, growing potatoes? I'm also going to cultivate them, albeit in a bucket! I just like to fantasize about myself being an old chap in a potato field, when actually it's just going to end up being me with a bucket of homegrown potatoes.

My objective is to meet people who work with potatoes in various ways. The dilemma is that there are just so many people who are passionate about potatoes. I've decided to meet one of Sweden's most knowledgeable potato growers, Andreas "Ante" Wiklund. Ante runs a large potato farm at Stora Tollby in Gotland. He distributes his produce primarily to restaurants and grocery stores all over Sweden. Respect! On the island, I also visit Matilda Svahn, who runs a small cooperative farm at Tjeldervik Gård in Boge on the north-east side. It's a small-scale affair, with a real love for the soil and the crops. Respect to her, too! They've helped bring me down to earth, literally, and given me a greater understanding and love of the ingredient that is the potato.

Stora Tollby

Ante's operations are huge, covering around 445 acres (180 hectares) of cultivatable area. He employs 13 people who work all year round on the farm, in the warehouses, and on the sorting machines. It becomes clear what a large operation this is as Ante is driving us around explaining everything. That said, the farm still feels personal. Ante and everyone else here works close to the potatoes and their development.

Cultivation and production take place from March to mid-October. Both new potatoes and potatoes to be stored over winter are sown in March and April. The new potatoes are harvested from the beginning of May until August. The potatoes to be stored are harvested from late August to mid-October.

The biggest enemy during the growing season is leaf mold. The fungus causes the foliage on the plant to wither, causing the potato in the soil to stop growing. If there's also heavy rain in connection with leaf mold, the spores from the mold go into the soil to the potatoes, which quickly go moldy, rot, and die. The biggest preventive measure against leaf mold is crop rotation. This means alternating crops each year and not growing the same crop on the same field year after year. For this reason, potatoes are grown on the same field only once every five years.

In Ante's case, where the production is so large, this means that he cooperates with other growers who get to grow other crops on his fields while Ante grows potatoes on theirs. In addition to potatoes, Ante grows other things on his own land to change things up.

Another way to combat leaf mold is to always make sure you have healthy seeds when sowing in the spring. Pesticides also need to be used (responsibly) because leaf mold still comes to Sweden's latitudes by air from more southerly climes. It's important to keep an eye on the weather forecasts to prevent the fungus from taking hold.

I ask about the environmental impact and how the control measures are felt in the soil. Ante tells us that soil samples are taken every year to measure the impact of pesticides, but so far no traces have been found. It's a balancing act if you want to be able to produce and supply the market with good quality potatoes in large quantities.

Organic farming also takes place on some fields each year. Here, they work with resistant varieties and pursue companion crops and crop rotation to minimize the impact of the fungus. The Nordic climate is favorable for organic farming. The organic varieties that Ante grows are primarily resistant to mold and other factors damaging to the plant.

Rainwater provides natural irrigation, but most of the water is pumped up from a manmade pond. Of the rainwater that falls, about half is taken up by the crops growing there, while the rest runs off down into the soil. The farm has drainage pipes to catch this runoff and take it to the pond, where it's stored. This is potato farming's life insurance. Without the pond, there would be too much uncertainty. With the pond guaranteeing the water supply, Ante thinks that sunny, dry summers are almost better, because then he can control the irrigation himself with the help of the pond.

Before the potatoes to be stored are harvested, the foliage is cut off and the potatoes are kept on the plant. The potatoes are left in the soil for two weeks to develop a skin. The potatoes are harvested using a machine operated by one person. The tubers are brought up into the machine in batches and the soil is shaken off. The last of the soil goes up into the machine where two people sit and sort out stones and other debris. Boxes are then filled with the freshly harvested potatoes, which are transported to the storage location, where the potatoes are put in darkness within an hour of being harvested.

When the potato came to the Nordics, there were no classic ground cellars. Storage became a big problem that needed to be solved and it remains one of the most important pieces of the puzzle in potato production. The solution is still "ground cellars." In the dark storage room where the potatoes end up after they're harvested, the ground cellar, the climate is regulated using the outside temperature throughout the fall and down to a constant 39 °F (4 °C) all winter as temperatures fall. People talk about the potato "falling asleep" during this period of falling temperature and darkness. During the winter, the potatoes give off heat, so you have to use the outside temperature to regulate the heat in the warehouse so that it doesn't get warmer than 39 °F (4 °C).

Ante tells me that the Swedish state ordered the digging of ditches and planting of fields in the 18th and 19th centuries. The ditches are still there and are a reminder of a time when poverty and famine plagued Sweden. Carpeting the country in agriculture was a way to guarantee the health of the population and a degree of prosperity. All the time, Ante wants to try and test new varieties to refine his production so that he's not left vulnerable by having too few waxy varieties. As I said, it's a large farm, but Ante is conscious of that and is developing it as if it were a smallholding. It's hands-on, mucky work all year round out in the fields. The potato demands it, and we just have to accept it.

Tjeldervik Gård

By the sea on the eastern side of Gotland, Matilda Svahn has a small cooperative farm. She has no employees but works with volunteers who are interested in the kind of organic farming pursued at the farm. The volunteers come from all over the world and stay an average of five weeks to learn. Food and accommodation are included. I think it must be incredibly inspiring to go to another country and learn in this way.

The cooperative farm is supported by roughly 70 households who buy the majority of Matilda's produce throughout the year. She grows, harvests, and delivers vegetables to Visby in boxes once a week from May to November. There's one box for each household. Along with the vegetables, she provides recipes and a nice story with inspiration for cooking.

Here at Tjeldervik, everything is much smaller compared to Stora Tollby. I feel this immediately when I jump on the trailer, and Dolly, Matilda's red tractor, pulls us up to the biggest field, where she grows most of her produce. Everything is grown organically and with roughly the same processes as Ante uses, but here the crop rotation is managed within the farm. On the biggest field it becomes clear to me what crop rotation really means. Not even half the field is cultivated, and I realize that it's not just about owning land and grafting away with the same crops in the same location every year.

After being with Ante, I'm struck by how small Matilda's farm is, but also how similar it is in many respects. Just like at Stora Tollby, Matilda plants her potatoes in April and she also irrigates with water from her own pond that stores rainwater. But there are also differences, of course. Instead of ground cellars, at Tjeldervik the potatoes are kept in the ground until it's time to deliver them. Only then are they picked. All the potatoes are delivered immediately after picking and they keep very well in the ground, so no storage is needed. I find this interesting, but I also understand that larger growers can't work in this way. The fact that potatoes can be kept in the ground gets me thinking about my own growing.

At Tjeldervik, the potatoes are harvested by turning the soil with a potato harvester. In contrast to the larger farm's harvester, which picks up the potatoes where they're then sorted, Matilda's potatoes are taken care of on the ground. They're picked by hand, placed in baskets, and poured into a wagon. It's a tough job, but many hands make light work ... well, lighter work, at least.

On the ferry home, I think about how to go about growing in my buckets at home. I'll definitely sow my potatoes in March and April, just like my new-found potato friends do. And I'm probably going to rotate my crops.

LYCKEBY
10 LIT.

Final words

I've been thinking about my buckets for a few months now, and what have I learned that's going to be important? Well, the biggest lesson is probably to keep it simple and not overcomplicate things. Of course, I don't take potato farming as seriously as Ante and Matilda, but for me I prefer to keep things simple. Especially in the beginning.

I start by sprouting the potatoes indoors. I put moist soil in a long pan and stick my potatoes in to sprout, which takes a few weeks and requires some patience. A black belt in waiting comes in handy here, which is something the professional growers definitely have. But waiting is really not something I go in for. Once the potatoes are sprouted, I pour soil into a bucket that I have made a hole in the bottom of so that the excess water can drain away. Around half the bucket should be filled with soil. I then put three seed potatoes in each bucket a little bit into the soil, fill with about 3 inches (10 cm) of soil, water them, and place the buckets in a warm place indoors.

Once the foliage starts to emerge, I put the bucket outside and (just like Ante and Matilda) make sure it's not exposed to frost and that the soil isn't dry. I don't have an irrigation device, so I'll just have to do it as I go. I have a feeling I'll need a lot of water! I try not to have it too hot where the buckets are so that the soil doesn't dry out. My advantage over growing in fields is that I can move things around. So that's one benefit of my growing method, at least! I water, protect from frost, and wait about two months before I stick my fingers in the soil to feel around for any potatoes. I've had varying degrees of success with my various varieties. Even my teachers struggle with the same problem, in that some varieties do better than others. My buckets are home to my absolute favorite, Annabelle, the loyal servant Bintje, Solist, and Amandine. Solist hasn't given me much luck, but I'll give it another try in the years to come. Fortunately, Annabelle did really well by midsummer and literally exploded in the bucket. Amandine didn't make it through a frost one night, so I got to experience the failure of a plant that died completely. It was sad, but a good lesson about how things turn out after a cold night. Bintje, on the other hand, was a stroke of luck. For some reason, the frost didn't get it, maybe because it was in a different corner the night that Amandine succumbed. I survived leaf mold, which was most pleasing and probably beginner's luck, and I got to feel like a grower from March to October. Although I didn't live with the plants every day, I loved my potatoes and my cultivation, just as I know Ante and Matilda do.

And it's here, with the plants that have given me my harvest, with Ante and Matilda in mind, and all the recipes, the history, and my life with potatoes, that I finally put down my pen and bring this book to a close. I'll take my Annabelle now, who gave me such a good yield, boil a pot, sit down on my own at the table, and get out some good butter and salt. I won't think about potatoes for a while and will just eat them. Thank you.

Recipe directory

Variety directory

Acknowledgements

A big thank you to everyone who has been involved and helped this book to see the light of day.

The team around the book:

Photographer Roland Persson, editor Elisabeth Fock, designer Stefan Fält, publisher Maria Nilsson, and photography assistant Erik Ögnelooh—such a great job, thank you!

To everyone working at the restaurant Hantverket, without you there would be no book, no life, and no context—thank you!

And:

Rickard Villard, Matilda Svahn, Olle Ekengren, Johan Björkman, Andreas "Ante" Wiklund, Jonas Petersson, Tom Sjöstedt, Matias Alcala Åslund, Stina Ekengren, Torbjörn Blomqvist, Jessica Ekengren, Henrik Francke, Pelle Bosta, Fredrik Juhlin, and Ella Nilsson—thank you for your support, for checking, for pointing me in the right direction, and for taking me down a peg or two.

And, my warmest thanks to the potatoes. Thank you for being there, for listening, and for always being so loyal. I'm forever in your debt and hope one day to pay you back. Thank you!

Never forget what saved you

What took you by the hand and led you away from hunger

May it always be close by

POTATO TOTAL

Timeless Recipes for Every Home Cook

Co-edited, texts, and recipes by Stefan Ekengren

Translation by GLOBALscandinavia for booklab GmbH, Munich

Photos by Roland Persson
Photo assistance by Erik Ögnelooh
Design by Stefan Fält
Cover and layout by Melanie Ullrich
Cover illustrations by Karthik Iyengar
Typefaces by Frank Grießhammer (Source Serif), Paul D. Hunt (Source Sans), and Arno Drescher (Super Grotesk)

Printed by Printer Trento S. p. A., Trento
Made in Italy

Original title: Potatis
First published by Natur & Kultur, Sweden

Published by gestalten, Berlin 2024
ISBN 978-3-96704-164-4
2nd printing, 2026

Die Gestalten Verlag GmbH & Co. KG
Mariannenstrasse 9–10
10999 Berlin, Germany
hello@gestalten.com

For more information, and to order books, please visit www.gestalten.com
Bibliographic information published by the Deutsche Nationalbibliothek.
The Deutsche Nationalbibliothek lists this publication in the Deutsche Nationalbibliografie; detailed bibliographic data is available online at www.dnb.de

This book was printed on paper certified according to the standards of the FSC®.

FSC www.fsc.org MIX Paper | Supporting responsible forestry FSC® C015829